The 6 Keys to Teacher Engagement

Unlocking the Doors to Top Teacher Performance

Cathie E. West

Eye On Education
6 Depot Way West, Suite 106
Larchmont, NY 10538
(914) 833–0551
(914) 833–0761 fax
www.eyeoneducation.com

Copyright © 2013 Eye On Education, Inc.
All Rights Reserved.

For information about permission to reproduce selections from this book, write:
Eye On Education, Permissions Dept., Suite 106, 6 Depot Way West, Larchmont, NY 10538.

Library of Congress Cataloging-in-Publication Data

West, Cathie E.
 The 6 keys to teacher engagement : unlocking the doors to top teacher performance / Cathie E. West.
     pages   cm
 ISBN 978-1-59667-238-3
 1. Teaching.
 I. Title.
 II. Title: Six keys to teacher engagement.
 LB1025.3.W418 2013
 371.102—dc23   2012050286

10 9 8 7 6 5 4 3 2 1

Sponsoring Editor: Robert Sickles
Production Editor: Lauren Beebe
Copyeditor: Laurie Lieb
Designer and Compositor: Matthew Williams, click! Publishing Services
Cover Designer: Dave Strauss, 3FoldDesign

Also Available from EYE ON EDUCATION

Problem-Solving Tools and Tips for School Leaders
Cathie E. West

Lead Me—I Dare You!
Managing Resistance to School Change
Sherrel Bergmann & Judith Allen Brough

Leading School Change:
9 Strategies to Bring Everybody on Board
Todd Whitaker

Lead with Me: A Principal's Guide to Teacher Leadership
Gayle Moller & Anita M. Pankake

Schools Where Teachers Lead: What Successful Leaders Do
John S. Bell, Tony Thacker, & Franklin P. Schargel

162 Keys to School Success:
Be the Best, Hire the Best, Train, Inspire, and Retain the Best
Franklin P. Schargel

Motivating and Inspiring Teachers:
The Educational Leader's Guide for Building Staff Morale
(2nd Edition)
Todd Whitaker, Beth Whitaker, & Dale Lumpa

Managing Conflict: 50 Strategies for School Leaders
Stacey Edmonson, Julie Combs, & Sandra Harris

Dealing With Difficult Teachers (2nd Edition)
Todd Whitaker

The Learning Leader: Reflecting, Modeling, and Sharing
Jacqueline E. Jacobs & Kevin L. O'Gorman

Lead On!
Motivational Lessons for School Leaders
Pete Hall

What Great Principals Do *Differently*:
Eighteen Things That Matter Most
(2nd Edition)
Todd Whitaker

for John Masters West

Contents

About the Author ix
Acknowledgments x
Supplemental Downloads xi
Introduction xii
    Special Features xiii
    Whom This Book Is For xiii
    Why I Wrote This Book xiii

Key 1 Create a Culture of Engagement 1
    Authentic Engagement 1
    The Attributes of Engagement 2
    Practitioners in Action 4
        Student and School Success Leadership Coach Q & A 6
    Culture-Building Strategies 9
        Share the Vision 9
        Get the Basics 9
        Be Resourceful 10
        Create Inviting Environments 10
        Monitor Social Relationships 10
        Nurture Collaboration 10
        Tune In to Personal Challenges 12
        Banish Fear 12
        Celebrate 12
        Have Fun! 18
    Wrap-Up: Create a Culture of Engagement 18
        Key Concepts 18
        Best Strategies 18
        Steps to Success 19

Key 2 Get Organizationally Engaged 21
    Exemplary Organizations 21
        Strong Leadership 22
        Strong Expectations 24
            Consistency 24
            Creativity 24
        Strong Evidence 24
            Personalized Data 25
            Personalized Data in Action 25

    Key Points 27
  Practitioners in Action 27
    International Business Consultant Q & A 29
  Organizationally Sound Strategies 31
    Capture the Vision 32
    Convey Expectations 32
    Just Do It (Sometimes) 33
    Take Risks 33
    Have an Attitude 34
    Engineer Adaptability 35
  Wrap-Up: Get Organizationally Engaged 35
    Key Concepts 35
    Best Strategies 36
    Steps to Success 36

Key 3 Engineer Engagement 37
  Perfecting Engagement at Faculty Meetings 38
    Participation Essentials 38
    Presentation Skills 39
  Practitioners in Action 39
    Education Consultant Q & A 39
  Engagement Strategies for Meetings 42
    Establish Norms 43
    Plan 43
    Tell Stories 43
    Clarify Purpose and Outcomes 46
    Invite Reflection 47
    Deliver New Information 48
    Share the Limelight 49
    Vary Presentation Approaches 49
    Access the Internet 49
    Apply New Information 51
    Assess 52
  Wrap-Up: Engineer Engagement 53
    Key Concepts 54
    Best Strategies 55
    Steps to Success 56

Key 4 Zero In on Best Practice 55
  Good Teachers Defined 56
    What the Experts Say 56
    Best-Practice Teaching 56
  From Theory to Practice 57
    Education Models 57
    Teaching Materials 58

Instructional Frameworks	58
Professional Development Resources	58
Key Point	59
Applied Research	59
Experimental Studies	59
Field Tests	59
Guiding Principles	60
Practitioners in Action	61
School Principal Q & A	61
Secondary-School Math Coach Q & A	63
Best-Practice Strategies	67
Get Up to Speed	67
Teach Best Practice	70
Identify Best-Practice Essentials	72
Adopt Core Instructional Materials	76
Power-Up Programs	76
Bring Frameworks to Life	77
See to Believe	77
Be the Best Model	77
Put Students in the Spotlight	78
Praise Progress	78
Wrap-Up: Zero In on Best Practice	78
Key Concepts	78
Best Strategies	79
Steps to Success	79

Key 5 Tap into Teacher Leaders 81

Teacher Leaders	82
Select	82
Prepare	83
Coach	83
Practitioners in Action	84
Lead Teacher Q & A	84
Teacher Leaders Q & A	86
Teacher Leader Development Strategies	87
Assign Strategic Tasks	87
Model	88
Welcome Different Viewpoints	88
Mobilize	89
Support	89
Encourage Risk-Taking	89
Highlight Results	90
Provide Incentives	90
Wrap-Up: Tap into Teacher Leaders	91
Key Concepts	91

　　　　　Best Strategies 91
　　　　　Steps to Success. 92

Key 6　Confront Change Challengers. 93
　　　　The Change Challengers 94
　　　　　The Confused 94
　　　　　The Distracted. 94
　　　　　The Discouraged. 95
　　　　　The Anxious 95
　　　　　The Coasters 95
　　　　　The I-Centered 95
　　　　　The Saboteurs 96
　　　　　Key Points 96
　　　　Practitioners in Action 96
　　　　　University Professor Q & A. 97
　　　　Subduing Change Challengers 99
　　　　　For the Confused 100
　　　　　For the Distracted. 100
　　　　　For the Discouraged. 101
　　　　　For the Anxious. 101
　　　　　For the Coasters 101
　　　　　For the I-Centered and Saboteurs 102
　　　　　For Every Change Challenger 103
　　　　Wrap-Up: Confront Change Challengers 104
　　　　　Key Concepts 104
　　　　　Best Strategies. 104
　　　　　Steps to Success. 105

Conclusion. 107

References. 111

About the Author

Cathie E. West has an MS degree in education and thirty-four years of experience as a school principal. She currently leads Mountain Way Elementary, a 500-student K–5 school in Washington State. Cathie has been twice honored as an exemplary principal, receiving the Washington Distinguished Principal Award as the representative from Douglas County in 1998 and as the representative from Snohomish County in 2005. She also received the Leadership for Student Achievement Award from the Washington Association of School Administrators in 2009. In 2010, Mountain Way was designated a School of Distinction for being in the top 5 percent of improving schools by the Center for Educational Effectiveness in collaboration with the Washington Chapter of Phi Delta Kappa International (PDK), the premier professional association for educators.

Cathie's professional experience includes teaching at the college level; directing special programs, such as Title I, Special Education, and Highly Capable; and coordinating curriculum and staff development for a variety of school districts. In addition, she was an editorial adviser for the National Association of Elementary School Principals (NAESP) (2002–2005) and a member of the Program Advisory Committee for the Washington State Leadership Academy (2008). Currently Cathie serves on the editorial board for *Washington State Kappan*, the Project Grant Selection Committee for PDK International, and the Communications Advisory Committee for the Association of Washington School Principals (AWSP).

Cathie is the author of *Problem-Solving Tools and Tips for School Leaders* (Eye On Education, 2011) and coauthored *Leadership Teaming: The Superintendent-Principal Relationship* (Corwin Press, 2009). Her writing has also appeared in *The Principal News* (AWSP), *Washington State Kappan* (PDK), *Principal* (NAESP), *Communicator* (NAESP), and *ERS Spectrum*. Cathie can be reached at cathiewest@comcast.net.

Acknowledgments

I am indebted to the generous educators, specialists, and consultants who contributed their illuminating experiences, time-tested strategies, and hard-won wisdom to this book. These sterling individuals include Lois Frank, Carol Fusek, Kimberly Barnes, Kelli Doherty, Tim Bartlett, Valerie Anderson, Cheryl Larsen, Linda Johnson, Tami Liebetrau, Robyn Ross, and Gene Sharratt. Thank you for sharing your superb craft knowledge and skills.

As for Eye On Education, when I signed on as an author I got far more than a book contract. I landed a priceless professional relationship with Bob Sickles—president, publisher, and editor. Bob was an inspiring mentor as I drafted *Problem-Solving Tools and Tips for School Leaders*, my first book for Eye On Education. Whether I was stuck for a title, wrestling with too many topics, or perplexed by enticing but conflicting themes, Bob subtly steered me in new directions or toward helpful resources.

The 6 Keys to Teacher Engagement, my second book for Eye On Education, has been guided by Lauren Beebe, a top-notch editor whose unfailing patience and spot-on advice supported my efforts all along the way. This book would not have taken shape without Lauren's expert assistance.

Support was also provided by the highly knowledgeable reviewers who critiqued my manuscript in the early stages, providing affirmations when I was on the right course and helpful suggestions when I seemed lost. The guidance provided by these dedicated reviewers—and their steadfast belief in this book—will forever be appreciated.

Eye On Education's production and marketing teams also deserve recognition. From copyediting to cover design, these talented specialists ensured that *The 6 Keys to Teacher Engagement* became a book I can take pride in.

Supplemental Downloads

Several of the figures discussed and displayed in this book are also available on Eye On Education's website as Adobe Acrobat files. Permission has been granted to purchasers of this book to download these resources and print them.

You can access the downloads by visiting www.eyeoneducation.com. From the home page, click on the Free tab, then click on "Supplemental Downloads." Alternatively, you can search or browse our website for this book's product page, and click on "Log in to Access Supplemental Downloads."

Your book-buyer access code is **KTE-7-2383**.

Index of Supplemental Downloads

Figure 1.4	School Staff Behavior Code	11
Figure 1.5	Staff Collaboration Exercise	13
Figure 1.6	Collaboration Exercise: Facilitator Guide	14
Figure 3.1	Teacher Presentation Outline	41
Figure 3.2	Professional Meeting Plan	44
Figure 4.2	Professional Reading Plan	68
Figure 4.3	Professional Reading Template	69
Figure 4.4	Activity: Formative Assessment = Changes in Behavior	71
Figure 4.5	Activity: Formative Assessment Test Item Options	73

Introduction

Improving school performance does not happen by chance; it requires highly motivated instructional leaders who possess a deep knowledge of pedagogy, understand the complexities of the teaching and learning process, and set the stage for improvement by communicating ambitious performance goals for students and staff. But even the *best* instructional leaders won't get far down the improvement road unless the teachers they serve support them. Improving student performance succeeds only when teachers are as highly engaged as their school leaders.

What does teacher engagement look like? Highly engaged teachers demonstrate best-practice teaching, use data to verify instructional effectiveness, make changes in their teaching approach when student performance falters, and dialogue openly about their successes and failures. These highly engaged teachers are professionally on fire and get solid results.

Every school leader wants strong teacher engagement, but how do you get it? I faced this conundrum when I assumed the leadership of a school with lackluster test scores and a demoralized, disconnected teaching staff. Although bright, experienced, and well educated, these teachers had become disengaged from the school improvement process—an endeavor some felt they had never been invited to join. As a consequence, the faculty's vision for the future was fragmented, the curricular goals unaligned, and the school's programs and services out of sync. Despite these and other hurdles—a student body shift from primary to K–5, growing poverty, larger class sizes, diminished resources, and high staff turnover—we set out to raise student achievement and year after year watched it steadily climb. In 2010, our school was honored at the state level for being in the top 5 percent of improving schools.

In the never-ending struggle to raise student achievement, I have learned a lot about instructional leadership. As with teaching, some approaches are far more effective than others. The strategies that paid off came from trial and error, extensive research on effective schools, and the exacting work of other school leaders who are making substantial gains in challenging schools across the nation. *The 6 Keys to Teacher Engagement* shares what I and other instructional leaders have learned about gaining teacher attention and commitment, engineering improved professional practice, and strengthening student performance.

Special Features

The keys to teacher engagement—and the concepts and skills that underlie their effectiveness—are presented along with authentic problems of practice, research highlights, interviews with successful practitioners, and helpful resources. Readers will get an in-depth look at proven practices and find the resources needed for successful implementation.

To help readers review, apply, and retain new learning, these helpful features wrap up each chapter:

- Key Concepts: Provides a bulleted summary of each theme's major concepts to help you review key ideas.
- Best Strategies: Summarizes each chapter's high-impact teacher engagement strategies.
- Steps to Success: Suggests activities that will help you put new concepts and skills into practice.

Whom This Book Is For

If you are an instructional leader—principal, vice principal, administrative intern, program director, staff developer—who wants to get teachers engaged in the arduous process of raising student achievement, this book is for you. You will gain valuable insights about ways to successfully involve teachers and find helpful tips and resources. The audience for this book also includes university and college instructors who are responsible for teacher and principal preparation. *The 6 Keys to Teacher Engagement* substantially supports graduate-level courses pertaining to educational leadership, school improvement, curriculum and assessment, and professional development.

Why I Wrote This Book

When I stepped into the role of principal several decades ago, school improvement was not in the forefront of education. There were no federal accountability mandates like the No Child Left Behind Act, no statewide testing aimed at measuring students' "adequate yearly progress," and no sanctions to fear should your school fail to raise student achievement. Since external pressures to succeed were near to nonexistent, improvement efforts relied upon the personal vision and drive of individual school leaders whose success varied with the level of support provided by their teachers. Regrettably, while some principals and teachers embraced the notion that schools could improve student performance, many did not. Back then, however, few educators worried too much about this. If student achievement went up—fine; if it went down—there was always next year.

The world of the principal has dramatically changed. Today's school leaders receive extensive training regarding their role as instructional leaders and are exhorted to improve *every* student's performance; reach tough school-performance goals set at the district, state, and federal levels; and close the alarming achievement gaps that fall along racial, ethnic, gender, and economic lines.

Understandably, principals across the nation are anxious to raise student achievement. To do that, however, they *must* elicit their teachers' support, and therein lies the problem. Improving student performance is an exacting business that requires determination, extensive collections of evidence, honest self-reflection, and the willingness to trade familiar but ineffective practices for new and improved ones. It should be no surprise, then, that some teachers fail to engage in the school improvement process or make only halfhearted commitments. Or that there are teachers who—perhaps because they prefer the status quo or question the efficacy of proposed changes—actively sabotage improvement initiatives.

I have worked with many teachers who fail to engage successfully and even a few saboteurs, but I have found ways around these seemingly insurmountable obstacles. I wrote *The 6 Keys to Teacher Engagement* to capture what I have learned for other principals—both new school leaders looking for guidance and veterans wanting to expand their repertoire of skills. The six keys provide concepts and skills that will help school leaders power up teachers' engagement in school renewal efforts, which will, in turn, strengthen instructional effectiveness and ultimately the performance of students.

I can't promise you that implementing the six keys will be a simple task, but eliciting strong teacher engagement isn't rocket science either. The strategies that support each key are sensible, practical, and doable. The payoffs are a deeper understanding of what it takes to be an instructional leader, teachers who are increasingly successful, and students who are making greater academic gains. What else will you gain? If nothing else, school leaders will discover that boosting teacher engagement is a professionally invigorating and endlessly rewarding career-long adventure.

1

Create a Culture of Engagement

> Raising student achievement needs to be the persuasive school climate—
> it needs to be alive everywhere for everyone.
>
> —Lois Frank

Student engagement is the new "big idea" for educators across the country—unless students are engaged they can't learn, and when students don't learn, they can't succeed. Nor will they generate the performance scores schools need to meet district, state, and federal student-performance goals. As important as student engagement has become, however, some educators think it involves nothing more than getting students to sit up straight, look attentive, and work compliantly on assignments. Savvy teachers and principals know that authentic engagement requires far more than playing the role of "model" student.

Authentic Engagement

In classrooms where student engagement is nurtured, students don't sit passively waiting for academic content to be spoon-fed, and they don't work in isolation on paper-and-pencil tasks. Engaged students are enthusiastically answering probing questions posed by skillful teachers—and generating questions of their own; collaboratively working with peers on intriguing projects; or intensely researching and then debating contemporary societal concerns. In other words, appropriately engaged students are highly involved in and responsive to the teaching process and yield ample clues as to the depth of their learning.

What does *student* engagement have to do with a book about *teacher* engagement? The characteristics that typify high-quality student engagement hold true for instructional staff—teachers who sit attentively at faculty meetings and complete reports on time may not be highly engaged professionally. We need to look for richer indicators such as teachers demonstrating—through words, actions, and results—a passion for teaching, a commitment to helping every student learn, and an intense desire to perfect performance (McEwan, 2002).

Surprisingly, although education is a dynamic profession offering trail-blazing research, innovative instructional trends, and fresh career opportunities around every corner, there is no shortage of disengaged teachers. Some are worn out from the constant demands that education presents or overwhelmed by personal challenges, such as failing health or family instability. Other disengaged teachers, however, are perfectly capable but coasting or, even worse, only marginally competent. Whatever the reasons, disengaged teachers stop growing professionally, become a drag on colleagues striving to improve, and are far less effective in the classroom (McEwan, 2005). Sadly, it has also been my experience that the classrooms of minimally engaged teachers contain a disturbing number of minimally engaged students.

The Attributes of Engagement

What exactly does "engage" mean? Merriam-Webster's provides a myriad of multifaceted definitions, but my favorite is simple and cuts to the core: "Engage: To take part" (2008, p. 413). Engaged teachers "take part" by teaming with fellow faculty members striving to improve and demonstrating attitudes, beliefs, and actions that strengthen not only their own effectiveness but that of their colleagues. These salient teacher qualities are captured in *The Nine Characteristics of High-Performing Schools* (NCHPS), a well-researched summation of effective school practices (Shannon & Bylsma, 2007).

The NCHPS authors grouped the characteristics associated with high-performing schools under nine domains, which are outlined in Figure 1.1 along with a few examples of the pertinent characteristics.

The NCHPS report includes "The School Staff Survey of School Characteristics," which my teachers completed shortly before our school received state recognition for being in the top 5 percent of improving schools. The

Figure 1.1 High-Performing School Domains

Domain	Characteristic Examples
"Vision"	• Faculty and staff have a common school mission. • Decisions are based on the school's goals.
"Standards and Expectations"	• Teachers are focused on the students and are dedicated to helping them succeed. • School leaders uphold a challenging curriculum.
"Leadership"	• School leaders are open-minded and take others' opinions into account when making decisions. • Faculty and staff are responsible for student achievement.
"Collaboration and Communications"	• School-wide collaboration takes place between grade-level teams. • Instructional teaming is used to plan curricula.
"Alignment to Standards"	• Teachers design instruction to build on students' existing knowledge. • The instructional strategies used are backed up with relevant research.
"Monitoring of Teaching and Learning"	• Extra instructional support is given to struggling students. • Teachers give students feedback so they know how to improve.
"Professional Development"	• School leaders support staff and find ways to help them improve. • Teachers are given opportunities for professional growth.
"Learning Environment"	• Students are culturally sensitive and respectful of others. • Students are given strong guidance on appropriate behavior.
"Family and Community Involvement"	• Community organizations participate in student achievement. • Parents are involved in the school.

Source: Shannon & Bylsma (2007, pp.135–137).

characteristics covered by the school staff survey are rated by respondents using the following numerical scale:

    0 = No basis to judge
    1 = Don't agree at all
    2 = Agree slightly
    3 = Agree moderately
    4 = Agree mostly
    5 = Agree completely

At my school, twenty-four certificated staff members—a mix of classroom teachers and specialists—participated in the survey, yielding a possible point total of 120 for each of sixty characteristics. The survey results revealed far more than I had anticipated, since the survey tapped into not only the performance attributes of my school but also the professional characteristics of my teachers.

The survey covers all the NCHPS domains, and the results verify that those requiring high teacher involvement—one through eight—are strong. The ratings range from 85 to 92 percent (Figure 1.2). What's more, the ratings for leadership (92 percent) and vision (91 percent), which correlate with strong staff involvement, are exceptionally high. All told, the ratings confirm that a culture of engagement has begun to solidify.

A work environment that fosters teacher engagement is at the heart of school success. In *The Six Secrets of Change*, Fullan identifies qualities that typify healthy school cultures: school leaders are open, ethical, and approachable; teachers feel valued; there is a shared sense of purpose; staff possesses the knowledge and skills needed to fulfill the school's mission; professional learning is ongoing; and the organization learns from its successes and failures (2008).

Interestingly, at my school, the characteristics in the school staff survey that best align with Fullan's school success attributes are among the most highly rated—the percentage of possible points range between 90 and 97, as shown in Figure 1.3 (page 6).

In sum, my teachers' evaluation of our school performance characteristics affirmed Fullan's observations—in effective schools, teachers understand the core mission, are highly engaged in efforts to drive up student achievement, and grow professionally.

Practitioners in Action

Every principal would love to see strong staff engagement, but that is not always the case. During the thirty-four years that I have been a

Figure 1.2 Overview of Domain Results

Domain	Number of Rated Statements	Point Status	Percentage of Possible Points
"Vision"	6	657/720	91%
"Standards/Expectations"	5	509/600	85%
"Leadership"	6	665/720	92%
"Collaboration/ Communication"	7	718/840	85%
"Alignment to Standards"	9	926/1080	86%
"Monitoring Teaching and Learning"	7	715/840	85%
"Professional Development"	6	637/780	88%
"Learning Environment"	8	843/960	88%
"Family and Community Involvement"	6	592/720	82%

Source: Shannon & Bylsma (2007, pp.135–137).

principal—leading diverse faculties at nine different schools—I have unfortunately encountered my fair share of disengaged teachers. What are the barriers to powerful professional participation?

To gain some insights, I tracked down Lois Frank, an exceptionally talented education consultant who works as a student and school success leadership coach for the Washington Improvement and Implementation Network. Lois provides technical assistance to school districts struggling to improve student performance. She helps administrators and teachers "analyze systems and structures, create a culture focused on improving student achievement, and develop an ongoing, reflective, data driven process" (West & Frank, 2010, p. 19). Lois's day-to-day job is a complex one that includes coaching superintendents who are striving to shore up district-wide improvement efforts, energizing work-weary principals whose schools are on the cusp of making dramatic gains, and supporting teachers struggling to boost student achievement.

I quizzed Lois about teacher engagement: How do you define it? What stands in the way? How do you get it? In the Q & A that follows, Lois shares what she has learned from working with hundreds of teachers and administrators:

Figure 1.3 Successful School Attributes Alignment

Percentage of Points Possible	Characteristic	School Success Attribute
97%	Student Achievement Focus	*Shared Sense of Purpose*
96%	Common School Mission Teacher Leadership	*Shared Sense of Purpose* *Staff Possess Knowledge & Skills*
95%	Goal Oriented High Expectations Staff Learns	*Shared Sense of Purpose* *Shared Sense of Purpose* *The Organization Learns*
94%	Instructional Leadership Leadership Integrity Data Driven	*Shared Sense of Purpose* *School Leaders are Open & Ethical* *The Organization Learns*
93%	Caring Leadership Effective Teaching Focus	*Teachers Feel Valued* *The Organization Learns*
92%	High Achievement for All Data Supports Professional Development Supportive Environment	*Shared Sense of Purpose* *The Organization Learns* *The Organization Learns*
91%	Aligned Curriculum Standards Driven	*Shared Sense of Purpose* *Shared Sense of Purpose*
90%	Team Problem-Solving Goal Oriented Professional Development Open Communication	*The Organization Learns* *Shared Sense of Purpose* *Teachers Feel Valued*

Student and School Success Leadership Coach Q and A

Cathie: What does effective teacher engagement look like to you?
Lois: I see engagement when teachers can explain the *what*, *how*, and *why* of what is occurring in their classrooms. I see teachers researching best practices for their own growth and for that of students.
Cathie: So professional engagement includes a strong student focus.
Lois: Absolutely. Engaged teachers demonstrate that *all* students are their responsibility and in their care: not my kids—their kids. These teachers refuse to give up on any student.

Lois Frank
Student and School Success Leadership Coach, Washington Improvement and Implementation Network

Degrees
Bachelor of Education, University of Washington
Master of Educational Leadership, Seattle University

Current Assignment
School District Facilitator
Highline School District, Washington

Awards and Honors
Harvard Principals' Center Summer Institute Appointment
Washington Association of School Administrators Student Achievement Award
King County Metropolitan Council Recognition

Biggest Challenge
"Helping educators slow down and become intentional and reflective. People often feel the pressure to do more and do it faster at the price of quality, authentic resolution, and clarity. They need to plan for intended outcomes and identify evidence of success *before* taking action on matters of impact."

Best Reward
"Being a participant in someone's growth and watching that person grow in confidence and skills and eventually become a change-maker."

Cathie: How do engaged teachers fit in with other staff?
Lois: They talk with peers and administrators about instruction, curriculum, assessment, and data. They share academic concerns and successes. These conversations are professional, collaborative, and constructive.
Cathie: So engaged teachers go beyond the classroom and see themselves as part of the school team.
Lois: Engaged teachers are *contributing* members of the team. That team spirit is a dynamic energy that "accomplishes" by bringing opportunities for success.
Cathie: Why do some teachers fail to engage? I am talking about not just weak or inexperienced teachers, but highly capable veterans who refuse to support school improvement initiatives.
Lois: Teachers believe that reform is difficult and painful. These teachers have worked hard to get where they are with lesson development, classroom routines, and management and now someone is indicating that their hard work is wrong and not appreciated.

	There is fear that everything they have been doing will need to be changed, that they will have to start over, which is overwhelming.
Cathie:	Fear certainly impedes any motivation to change. What kind of fears have you encountered?
Lois:	Teachers fear that they may make mistakes, be blamed, or be embarrassed. Some fear their ignorance of X, Y, and Z may be revealed because they assume everyone else is knowledgeable. Teachers need to be educated on the "why-what-how," to have questions answered, to be coached. But even then there is fear that they won't be able to do it.
Cathie:	Many school leaders share those very same fears. Is fear the biggest engagement obstacle that you have encountered?
Lois:	There is also disbelief that the change will be effective, attain the desired outcome, or be sustained. This is the challenge of good memory or, to put it another way, "We tried this before and nothing happened."
Cathie:	One last question: Given all the obstacles, how *do* school leaders help teachers buy into challenging changes?
Lois:	You begin by describing how the reform will benefit teachers and their students—making it clear enough that teachers will examine what they are currently doing and have already planned. More often than not, their current instructional plans provide a viable base from which new strategies can be built or inserted. Then in collaboration, you outline what the transition would look like as teachers implement change, identifying what is nonnegotiable to get on board. Culture is vital too. Teachers don't want to feel "done in," nor do they want to be led down a path without opportunity to examine the destination and the journey. I think that is true for any professional. Teachers need that knowledge to be prepared for what lies ahead and to be assured that when difficulties arise, "we" will work through those together. I also think it helps, when possible, to work on instructional change in manageable stages with frequent reflection and assessments of progress. Principals and teachers decide the indicators of success at the start of each stage, with indicators being data-based. They outline what support is needed from each other: teacher/teacher, teacher/principal.
Cathie:	That's it?
Lois:	Well, it helps to provide clarity regarding the intended outcome—often the end product is presented in concept terms and leaders cannot describe what it looks like. The reform needs to be *concrete*.

Lois's observations put the spotlight on some very human—and often overlooked—emotions that impede improvement initiatives. She talks about the "pain" and "fear" that teachers feel when confronted with monumental change. These powerful emotions are fed by teachers' memories of past attempts and failures as they watched the education pendulum swing from one reform fad to another. Teachers also want to be a part of—and even help lead—the change. When teachers are left out of the change process, they begin to feel "done in." Lois also emphasizes the importance of clarity—teachers need to see what the final destination looks like and get a road map that tells them how to get there.

Culture-Building Strategies

When school leaders cultivate a culture of engagement, they gain teacher buy-in and best performance. But what are the keys to engagement success? Besides time, attention, and persistence, school leaders need effective tips and tools, such as the practical strategies and resources that follow.

Share the Vision

What's important to you? Driving up academic achievement, creating a developmentally sensitive learning environment, exposing students to the fine arts, promoting healthy lifestyles, or *all* of these things? Your core beliefs need to be communicated, and that means over and over and in a myriad of ways. Tell staff what is vital at staff meetings, committee gatherings, and individual goal-setting conferences; create vision statements for your bulletin boards, staff handbooks, and newsletters; and spotlight your mission in your school improvement and personal goal plans. You will know you have been successful in communicating your vision when everyone—from custodian to crossing guard—can articulate your mission.

Get the Basics

Teachers cannot carry out the school's mission without the tools they need to get the job done. Basic materials include core curriculum textbooks and supplemental materials (at all costs, avoid requiring teachers to share items); oodles of shelves for books and specialized resources; ample file cabinets for confidential and archived documents; and state-of-the-art technology, like document cameras, e-books, interactive whiteboards, and computer projection systems. Discretionary funds for extras, such as professional books, instructive charts and posters, website subscriptions, and special project supplies are also appreciated. If you are working with a bare-bones budget, however, it may be difficult to fulfill every teacher's wish list. So consider partnering with other schools so that you can shave costs by purchasing supplies in bulk; share books, furniture, and equipment; and participate in joint fund-raisers.

Be Resourceful

Money has become so scarce in my school that we keep our paltry budget in the black by soliciting donations of copy paper, Kleenex, and office supplies. Resourceful school leaders are never reluctant to beg for additional funds and resources. They organize fund-raisers—I run one annually for student magazines, go after education and corporate grants, and request parent, community, and business donations. The tin-cup approach to financing education is time-consuming, but helping teachers become better equipped to do their job is the payoff.

Create Inviting Environments

Teachers are nest builders—they like furnishings and accoutrements that fit their vision of the perfect living space. I once watched an inspired teacher transform a cheerless, institutional-quality tutoring room into a cozy, inviting hideaway by adding natural wood furniture, handwoven fiber art, colorful rugs and pillows, and hanging baskets of airy ferns. Staff and students alike were drawn to this attractive teaching nook. Though I am no interior designer, I appreciate artful nest-building and encourage it by making sure the areas I am responsible for—school foyer, main hallway, staff room, front office, conference room, my own work space—are well maintained. Orderly furniture arrangements, colorful displays of children's art, and artistic paintings and posters not only appeal to the eye but create a soothing atmosphere where teachers can do their best work.

Monitor Social Relationships

Staff members require a congenial work environment—teaching in a Taj Mahal packed to the roof with resources doesn't compensate for a work climate that is demoralizing. Employees' social and emotional needs—to be valued, respected, and understood—are as vital as the physical ones. Ensure that staff interactions are caring and cooperative. This begins with conduct norms that govern how staff members live and work together (Figure 1.4). Always involve your staff when developing social expectations so that they will understand—and endorse—the expected behaviors.

Nurture Collaboration

In *Learning by Doing: A Handbook for Professional Learning Communities at Work*, team collaboration is described as a "group of people working *interdependently* to achieve a *common goal* for which members are held *mutually accountable*" (Dufour, Dufour, Eaker, & Many, 2006, p. 98; italics in the original). Teachers need to be "collaborative" in order to succeed, but what does that mean for *your* school? You can't nurture collaboration until your

Figure 1.4 School Staff Behavior Code

Interpersonal Relationships	Appreciate staff members' expertise and talents. Recognize that every job is important. Speak positively about staff members. Keep verbal and written communications professional. Respect confidentiality.
Climate	Be optimistic. Celebrate the school's successes. Support others. Look for humor and laugh a lot.
Professional Engagement	Keep the spotlight on student learning. Create opportunities for team-building and collaboration. Stay current with educational research and best practices. Grow professionally through goal-setting, workshops, self-study, and collaboration.
Decision-Making	Recognize that some decisions need to be made by the principal, superintendent, or school board. Seek input from staff members regarding decisions that affect them. Use nondivisive decision-making strategies (building consensus, dipstick surveys, trouble-shooting committees).
Conflict Management	Be constructive. Use face-to-face contact when expressing concerns. Employ conflict resolution strategies ("I" messages, agreeing to disagree, mediators). Let go of a past hurt—build a bridge and get over it.
School Operations	Do your part when help is needed. Arrive on time for meetings, listen attentively, avoid side conversations, use electronics as a meeting tool, and respect other people's opinions. Keep the faculty room inviting by wiping up spills, bussing dishes, and sharing treats. Observe school schedules. Conserve—accomplish more with less. Respect other staff members' property. Show consideration for classroom neighbors.

faculty defines it. Creating expectations for collaboration is similar to norm development: you must involve staff. Figures 1.5 and 1.6 (page 14) outline an exercise that introduces teachers to the current thinking about professional collaboration, provides opportunities for staff members to draw from their own experiences, and leads to a shared definition that will guide collaborative work.

Tune In to Personal Challenges

Teachers may be superheroes to their students, but in reality they are only human and experience the same range of health and personal challenges as anyone else. Health concerns may include physical disorders, such as heart disease, asthma, and diabetes, or emotional concerns like anxiety and depression. You will be better prepared to support your teachers if you bone up on their disorders through Internet research and consultation with medical and mental health professionals. In some cases, your school nurse may need to prepare health protocols for teachers in the event of emergencies, such as panic attacks, high blood-sugar levels, or symptoms of a heart attack.

Other employee concerns may be personal in nature, such as divorce, the death of a loved one, or a serious financial setback. Don't feel you need to pry into the private lives of your teachers, but *do* lend a sympathetic ear should teachers want to talk about their problems. Listening with undivided attention and empathy may be all that's needed to help staff members cope with personal challenges while on the job.

Banish Fear

Teachers should be held accountable regarding the effectiveness of their teaching but within the context of a risk-free environment. This may seem paradoxical, but the reality is that teachers cannot improve performance if they fear repercussions should they fail. When achievement data are scrutinized, for example, teachers with poor results should not be chastised but encouraged to reassess their instructional approach, connect with more successful teachers, and take advantage of professional development opportunities. Conversations about teaching practice between teachers and their supervisors should also be ongoing; this approach reduces stress and generates "more opportunities to praise a job well done or to address a performance issue before it escalates" (Farmer, 2011, p. 5).

Celebrate

Marzano has emphasized the importance of tracking learning progressions—the incremental steps students make toward mastering a complex concept or skill (2010). Apply this approach to teachers' efforts to improve

Figure 1.5 Staff Collaboration Exercise

Purpose
Today's meeting will involve staff in creating expectations for professional collaboration.

Introductions
Whole-group sharing: Name, assignment, earliest collaborative memory

Reflection Opportunity
Whole-group reflection: What connections do you make to the following quote by Roland Barth (2003)? *If you want to have your say, you've got to be present for the conversation.*

Outcomes
Whole-group sharing: In regard to today's meeting and mission, what outcomes are you looking for?

Collaboration in Action
Individual task: Read the following articles that the facilitator provides and highlight the collaboration practices. Be prepared to share any insights you gain from reading these articles.

Joan Richardson, "The Ultimate Practitioner," *Phi Delta Kappan*
Jennifer L. Steele & Kathryn Parker Boudett, "The Collaborative Advantage," *Educational Leadership*

Collaboration Attributes
Whole-group brainstorm: What are the qualities of exemplary collaboration?

Collaboration Defined
Partner work: Craft a definition of collaboration for the team's consideration.
Whole-group task: After reviewing the definitions of collaboration prepared by partner groups, create a final definition.

Wrap-Up
Whole-group reflection: What have we learned? How do we put collaboration into practice in our school?

Figure 1.6 Collaboration Exercise: Facilitator Guide

Purpose of Exercise: To involve certificated staff in creating expectations for professional collaboration
Product: Staff collaboration norms
Participants: Classroom teachers and special program specialists
Process Steps:

05 minutes	**Purpose** Today's meeting will involve staff in creating expectations for professional collaboration. Supplies: Individual copies of the Collaboration Exercise or presentation software featuring the same information	Facilitator: Read the purpose statement to the participants. Make any connections to previous faculty endeavors (e.g., developing a code for staff behavior) and current school goals (e.g., to become a more effective professional learning community).
15 minutes	**Introductions** Whole-group sharing: Name, assignment, earliest collaborative memory	Whole-group sharing (sitting in a circle): Participants share their name, assignment, and earliest collaborative memory (e.g., building backyard childhood forts with a sibling). Be prepared to identify qualities of collaboration that are revealed by the stories. Building forts with a sibling, for example, requires a healthy amount of communication and teamwork.

Figure 1.6 Collaboration Exercise: Facilitator Guide *(continued)*

10 minutes	**Reflection Opportunity** Whole-group reflection: What connections do you make to the following quote by Roland Barth (2003)?: *If you want to have your say, you've got to be present for the conversation.*	Whole-group reflection (sitting in a circle): Ask participants to make a connection to the Roland Barth quote: *If you want to have your say, you've got to be present for the conversation* (e.g., staff members should attend pertinent staff, committee, and parent organization meetings if they want their voices heard). Acknowledge each participant's contribution in a supportive, constructive manner (e.g., "Our new school staff behavior code should help us increase positive staff involvement").
20 minutes	**Outcomes** Whole-group sharing: In regard to today's meeting and mission, what outcomes are you looking for? Supplies: A beanbag or small stuffed toy, such as the school mascot	Whole-group sharing (standing in a circle): Tell participants that you will be a better facilitator if you know the outcomes they have in mind regarding today's meeting. Toss a beanbag or stuffed animal to individual participants to signal the opportunity to share desired outcomes. Participants should be encouraged to share, but may also take a pass. Affirm responses through paraphrasing (i.e., restating the statement in your own words) or amplification (i.e., expanding upon the comment while adhering to the initial intent).

Figure 1.6 Collaboration Exercise: Facilitator Guide *(continued)*

30 minutes	**Collaboration in Action** Individual task: Read the following articles and highlight the collaboration practices. Put a ★ by the practices you believe would be valuable for this school. Be prepared to share any insights you gain from reading these articles. Joan Richardson, "The Ultimate Practitioner," *Phi Delta Kappan* Jennifer L. Steele & Kathryn Parker Boudett, "The Collaborative Advantage," *Educational Leadership* Supplies: Pencils, highlighters, and prepurchased copies of the articles. (Tip: Save the articles for future readings and discussions.)	Distribute the articles with pencils and highlighters. Tell participants to read each piece and highlight collaborative practices, put a ★ by the practices they believe would be valuable for this school, and jot down any insights gained from the material. Article Sources: Joan Richardson, "The Ultimate Practitioner," *Phi Delta Kappan*, 93(1), September 2011). Order copies from PDK Online Store, www.pdkintl.org. Jennifer L. Steele & Kathryn Parker Boudett, "The Collaborative Advantage," *Educational Leadership*, 66(4), 2008/2009. Order copies from ASCD Store, http://shop.ascd.org. Allot 15–20 minutes for reading and note-taking. When completed, invite participants to share their insights.
15 minutes	**Collaboration Attributes** Whole-group brainstorm: What are the qualities of exemplary collaboration? Supplies: Chart paper and felt pens or an interactive whiteboard	Whole-group brainstorm: With the help of participants, list the qualities that typify exemplary collaboration on chart paper or an interactive whiteboard.

Figure 1.6 Collaboration Exercise: Facilitator Guide *(continued)*

15 minutes	**Collaboration Defined** Partner work: Craft a definition for collaboration for the team's consideration.	Partner work: Pair off participants (e.g., hand a roll of chart paper to a member of the group and tell *that* person to choose a partner). Then instruct the partners to draft a definition of collaboration using the previously brainstormed attributes as a resource.
20 minutes	Whole-group task: After reviewing the definitions of collaboration prepared by partner groups, create a final definition. Supplies: Chart paper for each group, felt pens, tape	Whole-group task: Hang the drafted definitions and read each aloud. Invite participants to identify the strengths of each. Then give one colored dot to each participant. Instruct group members to place their dot on a preferred definition. (Note: It is acceptable for participants to identify just a portion of a definition.) After this task is completed, help the group link desired definitions—or phrases—together to form just one definition.
10 minutes	**Wrap-Up** Whole-group reflection: What have we learned? How do we put collaboration into practice in our school?	Whole-group reflection (standing in a circle): Invite each participant to respond to the two reflection questions.

Create a Culture of Engagement ◆ 17

the effectiveness of their teaching. Track each teacher's progress over time on school, district, and state assessments. Celebrate incremental successes, such as students who move from level one to two on a four-point scale. Although these students have failed to meet standards, they are nevertheless making gains. Teachers will be motivated by your encouragement.

Have Fun!

I have always been able to find teachers who will take charge of "fun." These enthusiasts orchestrate campy YouTube videos featuring everyone from the principal to the custodian, all-school spirit days, spur-of-the-moment pitch-in potlucks, and relaxing after-school get-togethers. I wholeheartedly endorse these efforts by participating and cooking up additional diversions, like all-school pajama days, tugboat rides to offshore islands, carnivals, and over-the-top talent shows. Activities like these perk up morale and give staff a much-needed break from the wearing demands of improving the school.

Wrap-Up: Create a Culture of Engagement

Key Concepts

- Highly engaged teachers demonstrate best-practice teaching, use data to verify instructional effectiveness, and adjust their teaching when student performance falters.
- Improving student achievement requires determination, extensive collections of evidence, ongoing performance appraisals, honest self-reflection, and the willingness to trade familiar but ineffective practices for new and improved ones.
- Disengaged teachers stop growing professionally, impede colleagues striving to improve, and are far less competent in the classroom.
- Engaged teachers understand the school's mission, team with other faculty members striving to improve, and demonstrate attitudes, beliefs, and actions that strengthen their effectiveness.
- Successful school leaders describe how proposed reforms will benefit teachers and students, what the transition looks like as teachers implement needed changes, and the ways teachers can get on board.

Best Strategies

- Make sure the areas you are responsible for—school foyer, main hallway, staff room, front office, conference room—create a soothing atmosphere where teachers can do their best work.

- Provide teachers with the tools they need to get the job done.
- Be resourceful—seek out additional funds and resources.
- Enhance teacher effectiveness by creating clear policies, logical procedures, reliable schedules, and streamlined procedures for making service requests.
- Ensure that staff interactions are caring, collaborative, and cooperative.
- Support teachers facing personal and health challenges so that they can survive and thrive.
- Communicate your core beliefs frequently and in a multitude of ways.
- Encourage improved teacher performance in an encouraging, risk-free environment.
- Celebrate successes!

Steps to Success

- What are your professional expectations for teachers? List your top five; then identify the ways you communicate these expectations to staff members. Compare your communication strategies with those outlined in the "Share the Vision" section on page 9. Should you need to strengthen your approach, plan additional activities with a 30-60-90-day implementation timeline.
- To what degree are your teachers involved in school improvement initiatives? Rate each teacher on a scale of 1 to 5 (5 being high), listing what each has *said* and *done* that provides evidence for the rating you chose. Schedule an intervention conversation for any teacher whose rating is 3 or lower. This conversation should include a review of the school's mission, your professional expectations for teachers, and available professional development opportunities.

2

Get Organizationally Engaged

> Being an engaging leader means connecting to the organization in a way that inspires people, giving them the vision and purpose of the company and their role in it. These leaders enable the organization to strive for excellence.
>
> —Carol H. Fusek

Think about the word "organization" as it applies to schools. Do you picture hierarchical flow charts showing principals, teachers, and support staff or do you visualize school buildings, playgrounds, gymnasiums, and athletic fields? Or does "organization" bring to mind policies and procedures, rules and regulations, and the myriad legislative mandates that govern educators' everyday existence? I have learned from decades of experience leading schools that "organization" is not the people, the facilities, or the governance guidelines but a pervasive and powerful mindset.

Exemplary Organizations

In *Organizational Behavior in Education*, Owens and Valesky describe "organization" as a complex, socially demanding, interpersonal environment that "exists largely in the eye and mind of the beholder: it is, in reality, pretty much what people think it is" (2007, p. 185). This notion of organization as a mental construct may seem perplexing, but it is both realistic and encouraging. Teachers bring disparate personal histories, educational attainments, and work experiences to the schoolhouse; these disparate backgrounds yield different pictures of organizational life. This is not to suggest that fashioning a common organizational vision is insurmountable. School leaders have the opportunity to build upon their teachers' varied conceptual understandings and create the organization they believe serves students best.

Unfortunately, some educators suffer from the "legacy of the one-room schoolhouse," when pioneer teachers carried out their duties in isolation and by default had singular control of their curriculum, instructional methods, and learning environments (Glickman et al., 2007, p. 20). Although most teachers today work in schools with a principal and a platoon of colleagues, some prefer—as if it were two centuries ago—to go it alone. These independent teachers are often highly experienced and may even possess laudatory credentials, but because they are organizationally disengaged they hold themselves and their schools back. I have witnessed disengaged teachers—out of their desire for control or the emotional security that isolation brings—undermine their school's mission due to practices that conflict with current research, indifferent implementation of adopted instructional materials, and avoidance of collaborative discourse with colleagues. Individual teaching pursuits may satisfy personal needs but they are not professionally healthy for teachers or their schools.

In the ideal school, teachers are organizationally engaged—they wholeheartedly adopt the agreed-upon mission and embrace the work required to carry it out. These attainments emerge from a professional, supportive culture—as was presented in Key 1—and the three vital elements of organizational engagement: strong leadership, strong expectations, and strong evidence. When strong leadership, expectations, and evidence are firmly in place, they strengthen an organization's capacity to reach its goals. Let's explore these vital components one by one.

Strong Leadership

In schools, the governance style and authoritative strength of the principal determines leadership impact. You know you have strong leadership when every faculty member not only agrees on *who* is in charge but responds appropriately. If you think this is obvious, you haven't spent enough time in schools. People *other* than the principal are often in the lead. In my first year as principal, I unexpectedly found myself battling for the alpha position with a teacher who had all the makings of a first-rate bully and a cantankerous, overbearing custodian. I eventually won this leadership conflict but not without a few lively skirmishes. I learned that leadership does not spring from a positional title but rather from the potency of the leader's command. What leadership approach is most effective? If you think you need to become a schoolhouse warlord to make an impression, you couldn't be more wrong.

Northouse covers a variety of management approaches in *Leadership: Theory and Practice*, but the standout style—transformational—is more in line with Mahatma Gandhi than Genghis Kahn (2004). Transformational leadership "is a process that changes and transforms individuals. It is concerned with emotions, values, ethics, standards, and long term goals, and includes assessing followers' motives, satisfying their needs, and treating them as full human beings" (p. 169). Transformational leaders are gold—they inspire the people they serve, are highly influential, and become effective change agents. I have worked for a few transformational leaders and one remarkable quality they shared was their emotional impact.

In *Primal Leadership*, we learn from Goleman, Boyatzis, and McKee that the emotional sensitivity and outlook of managers dramatically affect the people they supervise. Managers who tune into the feelings of their staff strengthen understanding and build trust. Supervisors' moods are also important because they impact staff physiologically—cardiovascular function, hormone levels, immune response—and attitudinally, such as influencing the degree of team members' positiveness. "Even if they get everything else just right," the authors assert, "if leaders fail in this primal task of driving emotions in the right direction, nothing they do will work as well as it could or should" (2002, p. 3). At all levels you find educators—teacher team leaders, principals, directors of teaching and learning, superintendents—who are technically adept but unable to emotionally connect with the people they serve. What are the consequences? When teachers feel out of sync with their leaders, they may fail to assimilate their leaders' vision, a failure that in turn stifles professional growth, engagement, and commitment. Sensitive leaders tune into staff members' feelings and concerns and model optimism about the challenges ahead.

I recently witnessed a fresh-from-the-box secondary-school principal turn around the toxic culture of a failing high school within six months of taking command. For years this school was plagued by falling test scores, an increasingly discouraged and disgruntled teaching staff, and a dispirited, minimally involved student body. Unlike his predecessor—a pessimistic principal with a dour disposition and a dim view of his school's potential—the rookie radiated optimism. His beaming smile and infectious sense of humor uplifted flagging spirits. But that was not all. The principal set ambitious student performance goals in collaboration with staff; scheduled supportive staff development training; created new leadership opportunities for students, like coordinating community food drives and spearheading new student orientations; and arranged for student-staff culture-building events—from donkey basketball games to sensitivity awareness sessions to rousing pep assemblies. By midyear, the students and staff felt more confident and connected to their school. Teachers also began talking about how to go about improving student performance. They believed they could do it—perhaps because their principal had helped them believe in themselves.

Strong Expectations

Midway through my career, an eclectic approach to educating students became the fad. Teachers "did their own thing," to use an outdated but revealing expression, and no one was accountable to anyone else. Teachers dumped "basals" to make room for a hodgepodge of teaching tools they selected themselves; a potpourri of teacher-developed theme projects replaced workbooks; and student learning was not assessed but assumed—hey, the kids looked happy, didn't they? Everyone loved this way of teaching because expectations were minimal and—to be perfectly honest—it was so darn easy. Now we know better.

Consistency
The research on effective schools verifies that the work of every person in an organization affects everyone else and that instructional consistency—not diversity—is the key to improved learning. As will be discussed under Key 4, Zero In on Best Practice, consistency includes *shared* expectations about teaching and learning that are collaboratively set and consistently—there's that word again—enforced by school leadership.

Creativity
Does this mean teachers' creativity is out the window? Certainly not. There is plenty of room for teaching innovation and unique presentation styles—but only as long as parameters such as curriculum scope and sequences and school-wide assessment plans are followed. A good way to handle out-of-the-box teaching is by collaboratively developing nonnegotiable content, instructional materials (or portions thereof), and practices that every teacher will utilize. These must-do's strengthen consistency from teacher to teacher, grade to grade, and school to school. Key 4, Zero In on Best Practice, provides additional details.

Strong Evidence

Teachers are used to seeing achievement results by district, school, and department or grade level. This aggregate data sheds light on system-wide strengths, weaknesses, and progress trends, but rarely does it lead to substantive change at the classroom level. Some teachers may assume, for example, that *their* efforts have had nothing to do with a decline in reading scores, an increase in discipline referrals, or a high student dropout rate.

Performance data needs to be individualized before teachers find it a compelling force for change.

Personalized Data
Teachers find student achievement data more meaningful when they can compare their *own* students' performance results to those of other classrooms as well as to school, district, and state averages. You need not be a statistician to create personalized data presentations; in fact, simple formats work best. A few examples are displayed in Figure 2.1 (page 26).

Ranking teachers' results is another way to personalize data. By way of an example, Figure 2.2 (page 27) shows the ranking for fifth-grade teachers for math benchmark percentages.

Ranking teachers is a bold move that requires the right culture before implementation. In *Problem-Solving Tools & Tips for School Leaders*, I explain how rankings can be used to identify highly effective teachers so that they can *help* others, not demean those less proficient (2011b). Just be sure to share scores individually; don't reveal the names of other teachers unless permission is obtained first. In regards to Mrs. Vermillion, her results are strong compared to the district and state averages, but she could benefit from consultation with Mr. Cadmium, whose results are more promising. So arrange for Mrs. Vermillion to talk to Mr. Cadmium about strategies that could help her improve student performance in math. Teacher rankings, which can also be derived from interim assessments, core program unit and summative tests, and student writing samples, can help school leaders give a sizable boost to teacher collaboration.

Personalized Data in Action
Personalized data should be shared with teachers at a time that allows for ample discussion. Start by identifying teaching difficulties, such as a high percentage of second language learners or a new textbook adoption. This doesn't mean seeking excuses for poor results but rather pinpointing interventions that were or were not in place to address these challenges. English language learners, for example, provide their teachers with the opportunity to learn another language, broaden cultural understandings, and acquire new instructional strategies. A new text adoption offers the chance to consult with colleagues personally, at trainings, or via the Internet.

Spotlighting teaching practices that proved to be successful comes next. Did writing scores soar due to direct instruction regarding conventions, increased exposure to varied writing styles, or more discrete student feedback? Teachers usually need help isolating strategies that made the difference, and this is where the principal can help. Let's say, for example, that a fourth-grade teacher teaches writing first thing in the morning for 40 minutes, three times a week. The principal knows from access to classroom

Figure 2.1 Personalized Data Examples

State Assessment Results for Reading
Benchmark Percentages

Subject	Grade 4 Teacher A	School Average	District Average	State Average
Reading	89%	83%	77%	71%

Fall/Spring Computational Fluency Results
Benchmark Percentages

Math Fluency	Grade 4 Teacher A	Grade 4 Classroom Average	Grades 1–5 School Average
Fall	15%	25%	30%
Spring	70%	55%	65%
Data Point Gains	+55	+30	+35

Parent-Teacher Conference Participation
Participation Percentage

Parent Participation	Grade 4 Teacher A	Grade 4 Average	Grades 1–5 School Average
Spring	100%	87%	94%

Fall/Spring Oral Reading Fluency Results
Benchmark Percentages

Reading Fluency	Grade 4 Teacher A	Grade 4 Classroom Average	Grades 1–5 School Average
Fall	56%	60%	61%
Spring	75%	80%	70%
Data Point Gains	+19	+20	+09

Figure 2.2 Teacher Ranking Example

Grade 5 State Math Assessment *Percentage Meeting Benchmark*	Grade 5 Teachers
80%	Mr. Cadmium
72%	**School Average** Hue Elementary School
70%	Mrs. Vermillion
64%	Ms. Scarlet
65%	**State Average**
55%	Mrs. Ochre
64%	**District Average** All Elementary Schools
42%	Mr. Magenta

schedules and visitations that other fourth-grade teachers cover writing in the afternoon, twice a week, for 60 minutes. The principal should help the teacher determine whether or not improved writing performance stemmed from the morning time slot, the frequency of instruction, or something else.

Data that reveals marginal success or a decline invites the same kind of discussion. Why did science slump? Was less time spent on the subject? Did review and practice get shortchanged? Or did the teacher unwittingly skip essential components in the adopted science program? Questions like these can lead to a collaborative exchange that affirms practices that should be continued, fine-tuned, or dropped all together.

Key Points

Strong leadership, expectations, and evidence can strengthen teacher engagement and ultimately the school's organizational impact—but not overnight. It is an ongoing, multifaceted journey. Along the way you will need a tool kit of additional skills to enhance your leadership effectiveness. The leadership ideas in the Q & A that follow will help.

Practitioners in Action

Educators have gleaned vital organizational concepts from the executives of successful companies in the private sector, such as the ones featured

> **Carol H. Fusek**
> *International Business Consultant*
>
> **Degrees**
> B.A. American History, Art Practice
> University of California, Davis
>
> Certified Neurolinguistics Programming:
> Master Practitioner and Coach
>
> **Previous Positions**
> Associate Director Customer Service Logistics
> Procter & Gamble, Asia
>
> **Current Jobs**
> Company Director
> Valuable Skills Will Travel, Pte Ltd, Singapore
> A Resource on Demand
> Freelance Consultant & Executive Coach
> Asia-Pacific Region
>
> Company Director, Tirian Pte Ltd, Singapore
> Organization Learning and Development
>
> **Awards and Honors**
> Procter & Gamble Lifetime Achievement Customer Service Power Award
> Procter & Gamble Asia Supply Chain Re-Engineering Recognition Award
> Certificate of Appreciation: Invaluable Service to the Lao People's Democratic Republic as a Communities in Partnership Volunteer
>
> **Biggest Challenge**
> "In my career it was learning what it meant to *own* my career and not wait for rewards or recognition to happen. In other words, don't be Cinderella waiting for the prince to bring you the glass slipper. You find the glass slipper!"
>
> **Best Reward**
> "My greatest reward has come from the people I have worked with—people I have seen reach goals they never thought possible. It is gratifying to learn that I had inspired them to take a chance and pursue their dreams."

in *Primal Leadership* (Goleman et al., 2002), *Good to Great* (Collins, 2001), and *The Six Secrets of Change* (Fullan, 2008). Carol H. Fusek is one of these exemplary business leaders. She provides organizational consultation, executive coaching, and team development training for high-powered, multinational companies across the globe. In the Q & A that follows, Carol shares what she has learned helping companies improve their organizational effectiveness.

International Business Consultant Q & A

Cathie: What does your work entail?

Carol: Engaging with people who hold various positions in an organization—individually, as part of a large group, or small team. Ideally the contact is face-to-face but many times we work together as "virtual" teams. For example, I recently led a project via conference calls with team members in Singapore, China, Hong Kong, and Taiwan.

Cathie: Organizational development at the international level is an impressive mission—how do you approach it?

Carol: In each case, what is foremost is identifying the needs of the client and developing rapport and relationships that will foster collaboration and trust.

Cathie: You often support teams whose members represent different countries, races, cultures, and languages. Many school leaders share the challenge of working with diverse populations. How do *you* handle this difficult task?

Carol: It may seem daunting but in fact it's quite simple and only requires four things: keeping an open mind, showing respect, having a willingness to see things from the other person's perspective, and building trust.

Cathie: Good advice for anyone in a leadership role. But what does this look like in action?

Carol: It is important to do some work upfront by learning about your clients. It's a must to know what outcomes they want from my involvement and learn about their work experience and the roles they play in their company. I also need to know where they are from and what language is their *first* language. Lucky for me, English is the business language of the day, but often for participants that is their *second* language. So I must be mindful about the speed at which I speak, how I articulate, and how I use expressions that might be unique to my home country.

Cathie: Tell me about your training programs—how do you connect with company teams?

Carol: First, I avoid saying "training" program. I recall my first experience working with the director of a very successful organization learning and development company. He emphasized that we are not *trainers*, we are *facilitators*; then he explained that my role in an interactive presentation is to make it "inter/active." In other words, not *telling* the participants but rather *assisting* the participants in a learning experience.

Cathie: Is this where neurolinguistics programming comes in? It's a specialty of yours—how does NLP further your work?

Carol: I work with teams in a way that is more resourceful. For example, what we learn from NLP is that when people communicate they typically only share what is on the "tip of the iceberg," to use a familiar metaphor. We miss everything that is "below the water" and run the risk of not getting the full meaning of what they are saying. This typically leads to misunderstandings.

Cathie: Misunderstanding among staff members—and between school leaders and staff members—is a frequent problem in schools. How do you address communication setbacks?

Carol: NLP has given me a repertoire of questions I use to uncover meaning. For example, in a project meeting I was recently leading, I introduced a change that would impact how counter staff orders stock. I knew it was critical to implement this change but had to reach alignment with the sales manager who handled these counters.

Cathie: Change is hard in the world of schools too. So how did you gain the sales manager's cooperation?

Carol: The conversation flowed via a series of open-ended questions (Figure 2.3). My team got what they wanted and all I did was take time to ask questions.

Cathie: I like the way you listen and take into account staff members' concerns. It's a great way to build relationships.

Carol: Recall what I said earlier about being open and willing to see the other person's point of view? That's what I call rapport. So the first key is building rapport so that you can then build relationships. Now some managers worry about "getting too close" to staff; I tell them this–you are not trying to be their "best friend forever," but you *do* want to be able to talk to them, enable them, and understand what motivates them.

Cathie: With that in mind, how do you get buy-in when a major shift is required? A shift that impacts a vast number of people up and down the organization?

Carol: You start at the top. Said another way, start aligning the changes with the senior leadership and decision-makers; then let it cascade through the rest of the organization. In my experience, securing buy-in requires that staff know two things: the compelling reason for change and "What's in it for me?" meaning *my* team, *my* part of the organization, and *my* customer.

Cathie: Solid advice. Any final tips about organizational development?

Carol: Match strengths to strengths. Make sure a person's talents are matched to the right job—when people do what they are good at, they are more engaged and motivated. Then make sure people know what they are expected to deliver and have what they need to do their job well. Set them up for success!

Figure 2.3 Probing Questions

> In the scenario that follows, Carol, having explained that a change in ordering procedures is necessary, poses a series of questions to a resistant company sales manager.
>
> Sales manager: I understand what you are suggesting, but sorry, we cannot implement this change.
> Carol: Can you tell me more, what stops us from implementing it?
> Sales manager: The counter staff will *not* accept the change.
> Carol: What is their concern?
> Sales manager: Well, it's too hard and they do not like change.
> Carol: What specifically is *too hard*?
> Sales manager: It's going to cause them more *manual* work!
> Carol: Oh, so if it causes more manual work they won't support it?
> Sales manager: Yes.
> Carol: OK, so if we can design the change in a way so that it does *not* cause more manual work, would the counter staff accept it?
> Sales manager: Well, yes, they would be OK.
> Carol: Great! We will complete the design of the change and share it back with you for a final OK.

Despite working in a different field, Carol shares organizational strategies that parallel the ones identified by Lois Frank in the preceding chapter. When preparing staff for change, both Carol and Lois highlight the importance of relationship-building, clear communications, and unqualified support. Carol also demonstrates how persistent, skilled questioning can uncover the underlying reasons behind staff resistance. In the field of education, holdouts are often dismissed as stubborn, uncooperative, or just not liking change. What might leaders learn if they took the time to gently probe the reasons behind staff resistance? Perhaps, like Carol, who gained the cooperation of a reluctant manager, they could detect change barriers early and fix unsuspected flaws before resistance becomes entrenched.

Organizationally Sound Strategies

Organizational effectiveness is a vital but hard-won goal. Here are additional, reliable strategies to consider:

Capture the Vision

The administrative team I belong to drafted vision statements for our school district that capture the essence of our organizational beliefs (West, 2009, p. 29):

- Effective districts have coherence across the system.
- Effective systems have a shared understanding of powerful instruction.
- Effective districts work from data and act strategically.

Why go to the trouble? McEwan describes "vision" as "the driving force that communicates an instructional leader's image of the future and is based on personal values, beliefs, and experiences. A vision stretches the imagination and requires the ability to see the future in a way that others may not" (2009, p. 55). Our vision statements, which were reviewed by staff and then adopted by our school board, guide work at the district, school, and classroom levels. For example, the vision statements serve as a springboard for new teacher orientations, staff goal-setting, school improvement plans, professional development, instructional material adoptions, superintendent and principal progress reports, and long-range district planning. Take time to prepare vision statements for *your* organization—they provide an efficient yet powerful way to communicate guiding principles.

Convey Expectations

Organizations need staff expectations clearly spelled out. Most schools have a variety of written documents in place to support this goal, including staff conduct norms, faculty handbooks, student discipline guides, emergency manuals, school improvement plans, technology use agreements, and district policy notebooks. But if you think this type of documentation has got this expectation business covered, think again. When was the last time *you* read a policy handbook, goal plan, or procedural guide cover to cover? The reality is that written documents get shelved—or saved electronically—and lie dormant until replaced by next year's version.

To effectively convey or review organizational expectations, you will need an array of interactive activities. Here are several examples that are perfect for staff meetings:

- School Goals Data Hunt: Your teachers will need copies of your current school improvement plan and pertinent grade-level and school-wide data (e.g., state assessment benchmark percentages, oral reading fluency results, discipline referral summaries, interim test scores) collected over an extended period, such as three to five years. Working in teams of two, your teachers hunt for data that

reveals whether or not progress is being made toward goals. I allot 30 minutes for this activity plus additional time for team reports and whole group discussions.
- *Jig Saw*: Distribute chunks of a vital guide—the staff handbook is a good one to start with—to faculty teams. Each team records key points on chart paper and shares its findings with the rest of the group. The principal's job is to augment group reports with additional information and clear up any misunderstandings.
- *Jeopardy*: Create your own version of *Jeopardy* using important information from your discipline plan, volunteer handbook, technology agreement, or similar guides. Free game templates are available from www.superteachertools.com. Be sure to have prizes for the winners.
- Skits: A fun way to review expectations, like staff norms or procedures in the emergency manual, is to act them out. After assigning the expectations to staff teams, I usually have teachers create skits that demonstrate both the "wrong way" and "right way" to observe an expectation.

Just Do It (Sometimes)

You are not going to see many successful leaders making decisions arbitrarily. Smart principals, for example, wisely seek staff input and support before doing anything that impacts their teachers. But sometimes a judicious use of positional power is acceptable when it solves a problem, helps teachers, and gains beneficial results. Take staff meetings, for example. A well-handled meeting supports teachers' efforts to learn, engage, collaborate, and reach stated goals. Despite these benefits, I don't put the meeting schedule into the hands of teachers. I don't know many who would suggest giving up prep time for a meeting, so at the nine schools I have led I "imposed" weekly faculty meetings. Because the time has been well spent, however, I have never had to apologize for the frequency.

Other decisions I have made unilaterally include setting up parent advisory groups, shaving off recess minutes to increase teaching time, inviting community groups to participate in school events, permitting parents to make teacher placement recommendations, and leading all staff book studies. All these decisions had positive outcomes. I am not suggesting that sole decision-making be your operational mode, but on occasion—when you think the organizational impact is sound—just do it.

Take Risks

Teachers may work like Trojans to raise test scores, but if they are using ineffective strategies they'll get nowhere. I became principal of a school where teachers put their hearts and souls into an innovative math program that year after year yielded marginal results. Although I did everything possible to support their efforts—arranging for demonstration teaching, bringing in consultants, providing additional training—there was no sizable shift in student performance. Meanwhile, behind the scenes, I began investigating the efficacy of the math program, which had been touted at the state level for being highly aligned to state standards. If the alignment was there, what was the problem? As it turned out, the program failed on many best-practice fronts. The lesson objectives were fuzzy and there wasn't enough direct instruction, review opportunities, and skill practice. The curricular spiral from grade to grade was also weak, as was the alignment with state standards. Although there were topics that matched required learning targets, the cognitive demands—what kids were actually supposed to know and do—were out of sync. When I became convinced that the program was holding us back, I gave my teachers permission to dump it. Fortunately I had the backing of my superintendent, who didn't care *what* we did as long as math scores went up. Jettisoning the program was a risk—we would have no funds to purchase another program for another couple of years. Nevertheless, we set to work and pulled together a workable program using the supplemental materials we had on hand, "freebies" from textbook companies, and Internet resources. This got us through until we could acquire a research-based, competently designed program. In fact, in the interim our test scores began to climb. Lesson learned: sometimes risks are worth the risk.

Have an Attitude

In *Leadership Teaming: The Superintendent-Principal Relationship*, the spotlight falls on school leaders whose organizational attitudes convey an unusual degree of enthusiasm for the challenging work in their school districts (West & Derrington, 2009). The optimism of one superintendent, in particular, became a driving force that propelled his district forward. Despite a multitude of complex problems, principals and teachers adopted his compelling can-do spirit and readily embraced new initiatives. I kept this in mind when I introduced—with the help of several well-regarded teacher leaders—the Common Core State Standards (CCSS) to my staff. The faculty had worked hard over the past ten years aligning curriculum, textbooks, and assessments to our current standards—more than once, in fact, due to revisions. The newly adopted CCSS meant starting over *again*. This would be a definite downer, so I opened the orientation meeting with "We have an extraordinary opportunity to utilize all that we know about teaching and learning. The Common Core State Standards have arrived, which gives us the chance to not only build upon previous alignment work but to kick it up a notch. I am glad to be a part of this exciting work." The teacher leaders, who presented various CCSS components, were equally enthusiastic. Consequently, what the staff might have viewed as a setback became a professional opportunity.

Engineer Adaptability

I know a director of teaching and learning who regularly leads the charge for new instructional programs in her district. As soon as a proposed program is adopted, this director requires teachers to turn in the previous program's materials. If teachers fail to do so, she sneaks into classrooms over the summer to search for and remove requested items. Surreptitiously confiscating classroom materials is an extreme move that I do not endorse; nevertheless, it highlights the concern that some school leaders have about teachers' adaptability.

In healthy school organizations, school leaders help their teachers understand and assimilate change. When there are new program adoptions, for example, the usual one-day training provided by the publisher won't budge highly resistant teachers. The holdouts may require extended conversations with program consultants; proof of performance, like a rise in test scores from schools in the region successfully using the program; and visits to classrooms where the program is being implemented effectively. Side-by-side teaching with a peer or principal may also alter attitudes. When a major organizational shift is in the works, principals need to support reluctant teachers with credible information and authentic professional development.

Wrap-Up: Get Organizationally Engaged

Key Concepts

- "Organization" is not people, facilities, or governance guidelines but a pervasive and powerful mindset.
- School leaders can build upon their teachers' varied organizational understandings and create a structure they believe serves students best.
- Individual teaching pursuits are not professionally healthy for teachers or their schools.
- Strong leadership, expectations, and evidence strengthen an organization's capacity to reach its goals.
- Leadership does not spring from a positional title but rather from the effectiveness of the leader's command.
- Transformational leaders inspire the people they serve, are highly influential, and become effective change agents.

- The emotional sensitivity and outlook of managers dramatically affect the people they supervise.
- The work of every person in the organization has an impact on everyone else.
- Instructional consistency—not diversity—is the key to improved learning.
- Individualized performance data is a compelling force for change.
- Skilled, persistent questioning can get to the bottom of staff resistance.

Best Strategies

- Craft vision statements—they provide a powerful way to communicate your organization's guiding principles.
- Use a variety of interactive strategies to transmit organizational expectations.
- Employ sole decision-making when you think the organizational impact is sound.
- Take risks.
- Project a can-do spirit.
- Prepare for change by building empathetic and supportive relationships with your teachers.

Steps to Success

- What are your organization's guiding principles? Craft three statements that capture the essence of your beliefs. Collect statements from colleagues and teachers. What are the similarities? Do any differences help you detect organizational weaknesses?
- Do you have disengaged or marginally committed teachers? Schedule a time to meet with each one individually about their level of engagement. Present the indicators of disengagement that you have detected, such as declining test scores, negative talk, or the lack of involvement in school improvement work. Try to find out the reasons behind each teacher's organizational disconnect.

3

Engineer Engagement

> . . . we are wired to connect.
> —Daniel Goleman

I was a rookie teacher eager for information when I attended my first faculty meeting. I hoped for telling conversations about the bewildering art of teaching since the education theories I had enthusiastically embraced as a graduate student seemed nearly impossible to put into practice. The principal's agenda, however, gave short shrift to curriculum and instruction issues in favor of housekeeping concerns, like scheduling snafus, supervision assignments, and inventory procedures. I witnessed tuned-out staff members staring off into space, surreptitiously passing notes to each another, or doodling. The highlight of the meeting came when a supply committee was hastily formed after a veteran teacher scolded the principal because, according to her reckoning, red construction paper would run out well before February. I left the meeting vowing that, were I ever in charge, I would never run such an unprofessional and professionally disengaging meeting.

Perfecting Engagement at Faculty Meetings

In Key 1, "to take part" was the meaning ascribed to "engagement," along with attributes that affirm high teacher participation in the work of a school. Highly engaged teachers support their school's mission and actively work to improve not only student performance but their own and that of their colleagues. But how do school leaders elicit strong teacher involvement at routine meetings?

Participation Essentials

The following definition for "participation" provides clues: "having a part *or* a share *or* voice" (Roget's, 2001, p. 360). These descriptors are a recipe for success for any kind of professional meeting—give teachers *parts* to play, responsibilities to *share*, and opportunities to *voice* their opinions. Teachers can help plan meeting activities, provide presentations on topics of interest, give trainings, and express opinions through discussions, voice votes, and surveys. The idea here is to keep everyone involved.

Kimberly Barnes
Educational Consultant

Degrees
B.A. Education
Elementary Education, K–8
Speech, Grades 4–12

Career Advancements
Mentor Teacher
Instructional Coach
Dean of Students
Trainer of Trainers
Reading Consultant
Leadership Consultant

Presentations
Reading First Institutes: Alaska, Idaho, Washington
Washington State ASCD Annual Conference

Nationwide Presenter/Consultant for More Than 1,000 Schools

Biggest Challenge
"Helping people whole-heartedly embrace change as an opportunity to bring exceptional results in teaching and learning. Growth requires risk, and those in leadership know that we must change *practice* in order to change *results*."

Best Reward
"Seeing a district's shared vision and action plan being passionately implemented with every student, in every school, every day—then celebrating the results that follow in student learning."

Presentation Skills

Another factor that impacts teachers' attitudes and behavior is the way they are introduced to new ideas and practices. In *What Works in Schools*, Marzano (2003) presents in-depth research-supported instructional strategies that strengthen student learning: identifying learning targets, using visual representations, examining conceptual similarities and differences, providing cooperative learning opportunities, giving feedback, scheduling varied exposures to new ideas, and practicing new skills. These same strategies are equally valuable for educators leading professional meetings.

When there are new concepts to put across or skills to be learned, talking *at* teachers or showing them a mind-numbing series of PowerPoint slides won't get the job done. Brain connections for learning and memory need *repeated* stimulation to develop and grow (Ratey, 2008). With this in mind, school leaders can strengthen their presentation skills by using the same teaching techniques as their teachers. When sharing new ideas, for example, you can offer interactive opportunities to explore the new idea through collaborative discussions and authentic application. These ideas are explored further in the interview that follows with Kimberly Barnes—a highly experienced education consultant and staff developer.

Practitioners in Action

Teachers are a tough audience. Since they are constantly on the move in their classrooms, they thrive on action, so sitting through a tedious meeting or lengthy presentation is a trial. Teachers also battle for time—time to plan lessons, find instructional resources, assess student assignments, and collaborate with colleagues. Taking time out of a demanding day to attend faculty meetings, in-service classes, or curriculum meetings is therefore dead last on a teacher's to-do list. How can school leaders make professional meetings more appealing to teachers? Kimberly shares her best tips in the Q & A that follows:

Education Consultant Q & A

Cathie: You work as a freelance educational consultant—tell me more about this work. What do you do and whom do you serve?

Kimberly: I partner with schools to improve the quality of teaching and learning. My first step is to meet with school leadership and learn about their school's goals and needs, and then work together to develop a plan. My work includes leadership consulting, workshops, demonstration lessons, side-by-side coaching, observations, and goal-setting.

Cathie: You've provided training to thousands of teachers across the country. What goes through your mind when you are preparing for an in-service session?

Kimberly: Building a bridge representing where a school staff has been and where they want to be comes first. Then I think about the pieces needed to get there. Taking time to learn and reflect about my audience helps me decide how to best engage them. I also try to identify any roadblocks that may occur, such as mindsets, negativity, or philosophical differences, and then work out ways to break down potential barriers. Finally, if a school is not seeing notable improvements, I ask myself: "Is it the lack of a moral imperative to make things better or poor instruction?" In order to craft a sound plan, all of this must be worked out in my own mind before my fingers hit the keyboard.

Cathie: What steps do you take as you are developing your presentation?

Kimberly: Every school is different, so first I do my homework. There is nothing more frustrating than listening to presenters share information that is not pertinent to your immediate needs. I contact key leaders and teachers in the school who can share instructional methods, student data, teacher needs, and current struggles. I also ask where they are headed in the way of student learning goals. Next, I use an outline as a planning guide that begins with a success testimonial and goals, includes plenty of exploration activities, and ends with the development of action plans (Figure 3.1).

Cathie: How do you engage teachers at the start of an in-service session? And how do you keep them engaged?

Kimberly: I start off with a real-life story to capture the heart and the "why" behind the information that is about to be presented. Everything in education should reflect the faces of young people and the hope for their futures. Every dollar spent, lesson planned, contract signed, test given, and committee meeting attended should make an impact on real lives—futures being written. I am guided by this question: "How can I get this essential message across so that *this* in-service has meaning and is not just another list of things to do?" The answer is to make it real; to help teachers feel the urgency for change. So I talk about Rebecca, a second grader who made significant gains in math, or about an elementary school that met adequate yearly progress goals after years of diligent work in literacy. The next step is to get the participants discussing the students *they* teach. Only now are we ready for some *real* solutions that will help *real* students succeed.

Figure 3.1 Teacher Presentation Outline (by Kimberly Barnes)

Success Testimonial
From a student or a teacher

Presentation Learning Target
Goals for the participants

The Bridge
Where a school has been and where it wants to be

Who We Are
Student demographics, staff characteristics

Areas of Need
Achievement data, instructional approaches, curriculum, etc.

Proposed Plan of Improvement
Rationale for in-service target

Connection Between Presentation Topic and What Is Already Happening
How the topic supports current instructional activities

Introduction of New Strategies
Research, concepts, and examples

Practical Application
Exploration opportunities

Teacher Action Plans
Individual or grade-level

Cathie:	You are regularly called upon to present new instructional approaches to teachers—how do you find out whether or not you have succeeded?
Kimberly:	Success is determined by an increase in teacher effectiveness and that means student achievement. The classrooms that show greatest growth typically receive ongoing classroom-embedded professional development.
Cathie:	So workshops are ineffective?
Kimberly:	After a three-hour in-service most teachers will not change their practices. There also needs to be ongoing support

	through classroom walkthroughs, observations, teacher mentoring, collaboration, and instructional coaching in order to have true success. The one-time presentation is just a sprinkling of hope while the ongoing classroom-embedded professional development is an immersion into real solutions that address real problems.
Cathie:	One last question—what are the qualities of a highly engaging presenter? What do they *say* and *do* that sets them apart?
Kimberly:	A highly engaging presenter is a skilled teacher who is honest, respectful, available, and passionate about high-quality instruction. Top-notch presenters take the time to learn about their audience before arriving and to prepare a presentation that will be life-changing. The material presented must be applicable, so that attendees can incorporate the information into their teaching the very next day. The way the information is presented also sets skilled presenters apart. They give multiple response opportunities, just like effective teachers do in the classroom with kids, by saying things like "Turn to a partner and discuss how this information applies to teaching and learning," or "Make sure everyone at your table has the correct answer," or "Take a few minutes and jot down three ways you can use this information in your classroom tomorrow." Engagement strategies should be used throughout the presentation, such as think-pair-share, brainstorming on a Post-it, thumbs-up/down, discussion in groups, and creating action plans for applying new learning. Simply put: information and knowledge without application are useless.

Kimberly gives us tips that would power up any professional meeting. She knows her audience, collaboratively develops the meeting focus, and clarifies desired outcomes. There are also opportunities to discuss new learning, apply unfamiliar concepts, and practice skills. As importantly, Kimberly regularly checks on participants' understanding; she typically ends meetings, for example, by getting teachers to set goals and develop action plans. Kimberly incorporates the same kind of engaging teaching techniques that she wants teachers to use with their students.

Engagement Strategies for Meetings

Like Kimberly, I am responsible for developing meeting plans for a wide range of professional activities. In my role as principal, I plan thirty-minute faculty meetings—which have a school improvement focus at my school; school improvement work sessions that last several hours; and day-long staff trainings. I also provide professional development at the district level for teachers from different grade spans and departments. Regardless of the purpose, topic, or duration, I take the same approach. I keep teacher engagement in the forefront and strive to make teachers' time relevant, meaningful, informative, and practical. Here are key strategies you can rely upon:

Establish Norms

Meeting norms provide behavior guidelines for participants and should be developed collaboratively. Expectations should include arriving for meetings on time, listening respectfully and attentively, avoiding disruptive side conversations, and sharing opinions in a time-sensitive and people-sensitive manner (see Figure 1.4, page 11). Planners should include rules regarding the use of electronics, such as iPads, laptops, and iPhones. Is it OK to use electronics to cruise through e-mail during staff meetings? I think not. But before you ban electronics entirely, think about their usefulness as a meeting *tool*. For example, if Internet access via an iPad brings immediate answers to burning questions, then the value of electronics is immeasurable. So set parameters but at the same time be tech-savvy. Once meeting norms are agreed upon, they should be reviewed regularly and adherence periodically evaluated by participants (West, 2011a).

Plan

Thoughtfully plan professional meetings, whether it is a thirty-minute before-school gathering or an all-day in-service. Give the same kind of attention to your planning that you expect teachers to give to lesson design. Identify the meeting topic, purpose, and outcomes; create an efficient timeline for moving through the agenda; prepare resources in advance, such as copying handouts or finding the link you need for a YouTube video; choose the activities you will employ to engage teachers and get your ideas across; and organize participants in a way that enhances discussions and learning (Figure 3.2, page 44). It may make sense for teachers to work in grade-level teams; on the other hand, groupings that cover multiple grades might enrich some discussions. However you decide to organize your participants, think "teacher" as you plan, since that is the role you should play when leading a professional meeting.

Tell Stories

Research informs us that stories are more memorable than visual or auditory presentations, so learn to be a good storyteller (Marzano, 2003). For example, if I am emphasizing the importance of teaching a new skill multiple times and in varied ways, I might share with teachers my struggle as

Figure 3.2 Professional Meeting Plan

> **Resources Needed**
> PowerPoint slides
> 3 × 5 cards
> Common Core State Standards in Language Arts
>
> **Participants**
> 20 K–12 language arts teachers
>
> **Topic**
> Best practice instructional strategies
>
> **Goals (05 minutes)**
> Explain: Today's meeting has two purposes: first, to learn about and share professional best practices, and second, to generate and then categorize staff recommendations for future in-service.
>
> **Introductions (10 minutes)**
> Ask participants to share their names, assignments, and a childhood memory about learning a difficult concept.
>
> **Reflection Opportunity (10 minutes)**
> *Intriguing Quote*
> Ask participants for any professional connections they can make to the following quote: *The past is a foreign country; they do things differently there.*—L. P. Hartley (1895–1972)
> As participants share connections, make comments that convey the idea that educators need to continually develop their professional skills, which means doing things differently in order to improve student learning.

a young teen to master the art of parallel parking. My driving instructor—my courageous but not so patient father—had me practice parallel parking in a quiet neighborhood a few times just prior to my driving test. However, when I took the driving test I was required to parallel park on the main street of the town at the height of the midday lunch rush. As one would expect, I did not pick up any brownie points for my less than proficient parking performance. Not only should you tell stories, but you should also invite teachers to do so. At the start of a meeting about instructional practice, for example, teachers could tell about a time when a teacher helped *them* learn a difficult skill. When teachers share personal stories, it heightens interest and builds connections to your meeting topic.

Figure 3.2 Professional Meeting Plan *(continued)*

Professional Practice (30 minutes)
Encouraging Student Writing
Read "Big Dreams and Tall Ambitions in the Teaching of Writing," the first chapter in Lucy McCormick Calkins and Shelly Harwayne's book *Living Between the Lines* (1991). Ask participants to listen for important ideas, jotting them down as you read.

Ask participants to compare their notes with a partner and discuss the ideas they found important.

Give participants the opportunity to share their notes with the whole group. As they present their ideas, help teachers make connections to their instructional practices.

Writing Analysis
Show this narrative from *Under the Tuscan Sun* by Frances Mayes (1996, p. 3):

> Italy is thousands of years deep and on the top layer I am standing on a small plot of land, delighted today with the wild orange lilies spotting the hillside. While I'm admiring them, an old man stops in the road and asks if I live here. He tells me he knows the land well. He pauses and looks along the stone wall, then in a quiet voice tells me his brother was shot here. Age seventeen, suspected of being a partisan. He keeps nodding his head and I know the scene he looks at is not my rose garden, my hedge of sage and lavender. He has moved beyond me. He blows me a kiss. "*Bella casa, signora.*" Yesterday I found a patch of blue cornflowers around an olive tree where his brother must have fallen. Where did they come from? A seed dropped by a thrush? Will they spread next year over the crest

Clarify Purpose and Outcomes

When you identify a relevant purpose for a professional meeting, teachers' attitudes are far more positive. Teachers don't mind giving up precious planning or teaching time when meetings are perceived as necessary and beneficial. Several examples of well-defined purpose statements follow:

- Today's work session will investigate the reasons behind our unexpected decline in student reading achievement.
- Our staff meeting topic concerns a timeline for transitioning to the new Common Core State Standards for mathematics.

Figure 3.2 Professional Meeting Plan *(continued)*

> of the terrace? Old places exist on sine waves of time and space that bend in some logarithmic motion I'm beginning to ride.
>
> Ask participants to critique the writing style—what do they like about this narrative? Why? How would they improve upon it?
> Invite teachers to share how they teach writing style to students at their grade level.
>
> **Break (10 minutes)**
>
> **Teaching Challenges (25 minutes)**
> Common Core State Standards for English Language Arts and Literacy in History/Social Studies, Science, and Technical Subjects 6–12 *(available from www.k12.wa.us)*
> Give participants time to review Text Type and Purposes in the writing section of the document.
> Invite participants to share a writing standard that will be difficult to teach and identify the support they need from colleagues. Keep the focus on instructional practice as the discussion unfolds.
>
> **In-Service Recommendations (25 minutes)**
> *In-service Interests*
> Step 1: Give participants several 3 × 5 cards and invite them to jot down in-service suggestions that would help writing teachers

- Aligning grade-level expectations for classroom behavior is the focus of this afternoon's committee meeting.
- Our in-service will cover formative assessment strategies that strengthen student achievement.

Sharing intended outcomes is another way to enhance buy-in by informing teachers that meetings will be productive. Outcomes include what teachers will learn or produce. What's more, research tells us that identifying specific outcomes helps participants pay attention to and retain essential information. Figure 3.3 (page 48) shows some sample outcomes for the purpose statements listed earlier.

You should share the meeting purpose and expected outcomes at the start of every meeting and use visuals. Like students, your teachers have varied learning styles, and most will appreciate a graphic presentation of key points in addition to verbal explanations. This doesn't mean you need to create a PowerPoint for every meeting. A bulleted list clearly printed on

Figure 3.2 Professional Meeting Plan *(continued)*

> improve instructional effectiveness. Collect these cards and shuffle to mix.
> Step 2: Stand in a semicircle around a large piece of butcher paper posted on a wall.
> Step 3: Keep one card but distribute the remaining suggestions equally among the participants.
> Step 4: Read the suggestion you have aloud, tape it on the butcher paper, and invite anyone with similar or related suggestions to tape their cards below, forming the first category.
> Step 5: Call on participants who still have suggestions to follow the procedure in Step 4, forming additional categories. This continues until all the cards are posted.
> Step 6: Ask for titles for the various categories; when consensus is reached, write these above the appropriate list of suggestions.
>
> **Wrap-Up (05 minutes)**
> *What have we learned?*
> How will we put "new ideas" into practice in our schools and classrooms?
> Direct the participants to stand and form a circle. Toss a soft object (e.g., stuffed mascot) to a member of the group to signal the chance to share a response to the wrap-up questions. The respondent gets to choose the next person to share by tossing the mascot.

chart paper or large signs crafted via your word processing software will work as well.

Invite Reflection

When time permits—which for me means any meeting longer than 30 minutes—I include a reflection opportunity, using pertinent quotes that engage participants by amusing, inspiring, or inviting reflection on professional practice. Here are a few favorites:

- Roland S. Barth on culture and relationships: "Our strengths can become our weaknesses" (2003, p. 27).
- Theodore Roosevelt on financial setbacks: "Do what you can, with what you have, where you are" (Peter, 1977, p. 37).
- Thomas J. Sergiovanni on professional engagement: "What is rewarding gets done" (1992, p. 59).

Figure 3.3 Meeting Purpose Statements and Outcomes

Purpose Statement	Intended Outcomes
Today's work session will investigate the reasons behind our unexpected decline in student reading achievement.	Listing variables that impact reading progress. Identifying reading strengths and weaknesses based upon state assessment results from the past five years.
Our staff meeting topic concerns a timeline for transitioning to the new Common Core State Standards for mathematics.	Learning how the new math standards compare to current state learning targets. Creating a month-by-month timeline for aligning and implementing the new math standards.
Aligning grade-level expectations for classroom behavior is the focus of this afternoon's committee meeting.	Identifying behavior expectations that are the same or similar across grade levels. Flagging behavior expectations that invite further discussion.
Our in-service will cover assessment strategies that strengthen student achievement.	Learning three types of classroom assessments and how to use them effectively. Recalling three uses for assessment and how they impact grading.

Give participants time to read and think about the quote; then either do a go-around, calling on all participants to share their reactions, or ask for volunteers. Quotes are fun to use and powerful; they immediately get people talking and connecting to your meeting theme.

Deliver New Information

For most teachers, keeping up with professional reading is hard to fit in, given their jam-packed daily schedule, participation in after-school events, and family responsibilities at home. Consequently, teachers can quickly become professionally out of date. Attending workshops and conferences can help teachers stay professionally afloat, but state and school-district budget cuts have made dollars for in-service scarce. You can expand your teachers' professional knowledge by sharing key concepts from the articles, books, and web sources *you* are reading. Take time at faculty and committee meetings to give a book talk, share research findings from an article, or show an informative best-practice presentation from a website. A word of caution: Should you come across material you want to copy for your teachers, make sure you follow copyright laws governing fair use (www.coypyright.gov) or get permission from the copyright holders, such as the authors or publishers.

Share the Limelight

Your faculty is a rich source of instructional experts who can liven up professional meetings by demonstrating technology tools, sharing teaching materials they have developed, and modeling best practices. I have called upon teachers, for example, to demonstrate how to incorporate video streaming into lessons; access math, reading, and writing resource websites; use free online software to track student progress; and explain the cognitive demands associated with new curriculum standards. There is nothing more powerful than teachers teaching teachers.

Vary Presentation Approaches

Engaging teachers is akin to engaging students. Teachers have multiple learning modalities too and benefit from a variety of approaches—verbal, visual, and kinesthetic. Like students, teachers are also drawn to novelty and tune out when the same approach is repeatedly employed. Thus, when you are designing meetings, vary things for your participants by including activities that are visual or tactile or invite collaboration, such as the ones in Figure 3.4 (page 50).

Protocols provide additional ways to structure meeting interactions. A protocol might ask participants, for example, to form triads and share reactions to a new reform initiative. The listeners must paraphrase back—without critiquing—what they have heard. This simple protocol—which requires staff members to attentively listen to each another—packs an impressive punch. Just *listening* is a rare gift that broadens understanding and builds trust. Protocols can be used to delve into reading material, debate provocative issues, and share viewpoints. The best can be found in *The Power of Protocols: An Educator's Guide to Better Practice* (McDonald et al., 2003) and at no cost from the National School Reform Faculty (www.nsrf-harmony.org) and *Visible Thinking* (www.pz.harvard.edu) websites.

Access the Internet

Many powerful websites can boost instructional effectiveness, so don't hesitate to use staff meeting time to cruise through these dynamite resources.

Figure 3.4 Meeting Activity Options

Activity	Description	Example
Warm-up	An individual task completed by participants while waiting for a meeting to begin.	List three ways you have boosted student engagement this week. Share with your neighbor.
Entry slips	A quiz, question, or task that asks participants to recall or reflect upon information presented at a previous meeting.	On one of the 3 × 5 cards on your table, list the three types of assessment that were introduced at our last meeting. Compare your recollection with your table group.
Categorization	Sorting tasks that cause participants to think about and discuss concepts, skills, ideas, or other information.	Each of you has a bundle of cards with the attributes from our instructional frameworks. Sort the attributes under the appropriate framework heading listed on your worksheet.
Postering	A visual, nonlinguistic representation of an idea, message, or reflection.	Working with your table group, create a poster that illustrates the concept of collaboration.
Skits	Role plays developed by participants that illustrate an expectation, big idea, or skill.	Create a scenario that depicts an alarming violation of our code of conduct expectation for constructive problem-solving. Be prepared to act it out.

The following, for example, are aimed at Common Core State Standards implementation:

- Achieve the Core: Free articles, research information, and teaching tools (www.achievethecore.org)
- Teaching Channel: Videos of classroom teaching that support CCSS implementation (www.teachingchannel.org)
- ASCD Educore: Introduction to CCSS, literacy and math teaching tools, transition management (http://educore.ascd.org)

Figure 3.4 Meeting Activity Options *(continued)*

Pair share	An opportunity for two participants to share an idea, experience, challenge, or accomplishment.	Pair up with a staff member you need to know better; share your most rewarding teaching experience and how you made it happen.
Visual voting	Also called "voting with your feet," an activity that asks participants to move to a spot in the room to indicate a personal or professional connection, signal an opinion, or demonstrate approval (or nonapproval) or preference.	By what percent can we raise math scores? Vote with your feet: Move north: 5 percent Move south: 10 percent Move east: 15 percent Move west: Other Explain your thinking to your group and be ready to share.
Exit slips	A question that requires participants to demonstrate understanding of one or more concepts presented during the meeting.	On the exit slips provided, explain why it is a good idea to curtail student callouts during direct instruction. Drop the slip in the basket by the door as you exit.

We are fortunate to have a computer lab at my school so we can explore websites like these together. Not surprisingly, using the Internet to obtain information is a highly engaging way to get your staff tuned in to new ideas.

Apply New Information

Professional meetings where noninteractive presentations predominate won't bring changes in teacher behavior. As much as teachers appreciate hearing new ideas, they need opportunities to try out innovations before they feel secure enough to implement them in their classrooms. Built-in meeting time allows teachers to work with colleagues on tasks that will help move new ideas into practice. If you are considering a rubric approach to grading, for example, create time for teachers to use the rubric with authentic student papers from their own classrooms. This kind of experience, coupled with collaborative discussions with colleagues, provides the foundation for change.

Assess

Just like a good teacher, you need to check to see if you are getting your ideas across. You can assess participant understanding by calling on individuals or table groups to reteach a concept; monitoring pair-share and team discussions; and giving pop quizzes, worksheets, and small projects to complete. I have also used entry and exit slips to check on my teachers' recall of concepts we have encountered during book studies. A recent staff meeting entry task, for example, asked teachers to explain—in writing—seven concepts selected from *Formative Assessment and Standards Based Grading*: "learning progressions; instructional feed-back; and formative, obtrusive, unobtrusive, student generated, and summative assessments" (Marzano, 2010, pp. 10–31). We had studied these concepts several months earlier and I wanted to find out what the staff remembered. I learned that retention was very strong for five of the seven concepts but fuzzy in regard to learning progressions and unobtrusive assessments. As a result, I revisited these vital assessment ideas at the very next faculty meeting. Whichever avenue you choose for assessment, be sure to affirm appropriate responses, correct errors, and reteach when necessary.

Wrap-Up: Engineer Engagement

Key Concepts

- High teacher engagement is verified by high teacher involvement in the work of the school.
- Teachers need parts to play, responsibilities to share, and opportunities to voice their opinions.
- School leaders who forge a positive emotional connection with the people they supervise become effective change agents.
- When leaders become overly demanding or disregard feelings, staff members may retreat rather than embrace new challenges.
- *How* school leaders share new ideas and approaches with their teachers is as important as *what* is shared. School leaders should use the same teaching practices that they expect their teachers to use.
- Leaders who tune in to their staff—paying attention to emotions, values, and needs—are able to transform the individuals they serve.
- Teacher meetings should have a professional focus and contribute to the improvement.

Best Strategies

- Encourage professional behavior at meetings by creating and using well-developed participation norms.
- Plan professional meetings as carefully as you expect your teachers to plan their lessons.
- Use stories to illustrate important concepts and pique participant interest.
- Boost teacher engagement by identifying the purpose and expected outcomes for every meeting.
- Create reflection opportunities by sharing quotes that help teachers make personal or professional connections to your meeting topic.
- Be a good teacher—share articles, text excerpts, web resources, and research findings with your staff on a regular basis.
- Put the spotlight on teacher leaders by recruiting them for faculty, in-service, and committee meeting presentations.
- Kick your meetings up a notch by including engaging activities and collaborative conversations.
- Give your teachers application opportunities by giving them time during meetings to try out new ideas.

Steps to Success

- Design a series of staff meetings that cover a topic of importance to you and your teachers. Identify purpose and intended outcomes; then choose engagement activities (e.g., entry slips, skits, pair-share); resources (e.g., articles, videos); and participant organizational models (e.g., grade-level groups, whole-faculty discussion). Create a realistic timeline for getting through your agenda.
- Review the topics of the meetings that you have scheduled for the next six months and search for quotes that will engage and inspire your staff or invite professional reflection. Sources for quotes include professional books and journals, biographies of noteworthy leaders in education and related fields, and nonfiction material from magazines, newspapers, and the Internet.

4

Zero In on Best Practice

> The only way to improve educational practice is to approach educational innovation with . . . a deliberate, measured sense of its worth.
> —Arthur K. Ellis

Although the education community has coalesced around the concept of "best practice," this effort has been unwittingly undermined by the long-standing, heartfelt belief in the power of the "good teacher." You will often hear comments like these:

> Curriculum director: "A good teacher can make *any* program work."
> Principal: "They're good teachers—I just stay out of their way."
> Teacher: "I'm a good teacher—no one needs to tell me what or how to teach."

Based on such repeated comments, you would think that good teaching is a mystical art known only to the practitioners and that the notion of best practice is not only ill conceived, but unwise. The literature on teaching effectiveness clearly states otherwise; but before we investigate best practice, let's pin down the qualities of "good teachers."

Good Teachers Defined

At the start of my supervisory career, teachers had to possess just a few attributes to merit the prized designation "good teacher." Good teachers had strong organizational skills; effective student management techniques—no student disruptions or rude talk here; and dazzling presentation styles—these teachers were just plain fun to watch. These were the teachers whose instructional materials were at their fingertips; whose grades were turned in on time; and whose uncluttered classrooms were irresistibly appealing. I naively assumed that if teachers maintained student interest, kept their classes under control, and organized themselves and their environment that teaching—*any* kind of teaching—would do. Now I know better—a good teacher must possess a complexity of characteristics and a wide range of instructional practices if students are to succeed.

What the Experts Say

In her well-researched book *10 Traits of Highly Effective Teachers*, Elaine McEwan identifies individual, instructional, and cognitive qualities that set good teachers apart from their peers (2002). McEwan's highly effective teachers are knowledgeable, highly skilled, goal-oriented, student-centered, and engaging. What's more, they get results—students learn.

Robert Marzano also emphasizes the importance of teaching effectiveness and homes in on several essential teaching elements that support student achievement, such as feedback that verifies students' depth of knowledge acquisition, "instructional strategies, classroom management, and classroom curriculum design" (2003, p. 77). Each of the foregoing elements is critical, Marzano emphasizes, but curricular design is especially important as it encompasses teachers' day-to-day decisions about what to teach, such as making predictions in reading; the learning activities employed as lessons unfold, such as sharing predictions with a partner; and the opportunities provided for practice, such as applying prediction-making skills to stories written by students.

Obviously, there is more to being a good teacher than demonstrating a commanding, compelling, and controlled presence in the classroom. Good teachers must be knowledgeable about the subjects they teach, thoughtful about lesson design and learning activities, skillful instructional strategists, and savvy assessors of student progress. Which gets us right back to best-practice teaching—what does *that* look like in action?

Best-Practice Teaching

Type "best teaching practices" into your favorite search engine and nearly a hundred thousand sites will pop up. This impressive result stems from decades of interest in how people learn and extensive research in fields

Figure 4.1 Learning Theories

Theory	Streamlined Explanation
Behaviorism	Behavior results from conditioning.
Constructivism	Knowledge is gained from interactions with ideas and experiences.
Developmental growth stages	Maturation coupled with experience yields growth, such as in intelligence.
Experiential learning	Children learn by doing.
Multiple intelligences	Cognitive ability is not singular but comes in a wide variety of forms.
Social group dynamics	Group collaboration is generally more productive than individual effort.

such as sociology, psychology, anthropology, linguistics, the neurosciences, medicine, and human development. This research precipitated countless learning theories, including the ones listed in Figure 4.1.

The foregoing learning theories are by no means the only ones to emerge, but they are certainly the ones most familiar to educators. A learning theory doesn't make much of an impact on the education scene, however, until it moves into practice.

From Theory to Practice

Some learning theories became the basis for education models, teaching materials, instructional frameworks, and professional development resources that have been implemented in schools throughout the United States. The information that follows provides examples of the various ways theory moves into practice.

Education Models

An education model provides a teaching philosophy—a cluster of beliefs about what works best—that is based upon selected learning theories. This philosophy is usually coupled with specific strategies for presenting curriculum concepts and skills to students. The following models became popular, at varying times, between the 1930s and 1990s: sight word reading, whole language, phonics reading, new math, inquiry-based science, mastery learning, outcome-based education (OBE), direct instruction, instructional theory into practice (ITIP), cooperative learning, critical thinking skills, and curriculum integration. Interestingly, these models are still present—in one form or another—in schools today. They have been joined, however, by a flurry of additional approaches such as response to intervention (RTI), brain-compatible instruction, digital teaching, social thinking, and differentiated instruction, to name just a few.

Teaching Materials

Publishers of educational materials—textbooks, workbooks, software, CDs and DVDs, and activity kits—hire experts well versed in learning theory to design their products. Many published programs spiral from grade to grade, such as kindergarten through grade eight, and come with a variety of supplemental materials. A math program, for example, might augment the teacher guide and student text with tubs of manipulative materials, such as counters and unifix cubes; DVDs of model lessons; and CDs of copy-ready tests.

Instructional Frameworks

There is no shortage of instructional frameworks—think "teaching guides"—that have been developed by education leaders, universities, consultancy groups, school districts, and state departments of education. Charlotte Danielson's version—*The Framework for Teaching*—is familiar to most educators (2007). Danielson's framework is aligned to the Interstate New Teacher Assessment and Support Consortium standards and provides teachers with expectations for designing lessons, creating the affective and physical learning environments, teaching and assessing students, and meeting a variety of professional obligations (www.danielsongroup.org). There are other frameworks besides Danielson's, however, such as *The Marzano Teacher Evaluation Model* (www.tepep-wa.org), based upon Robert Marzano's (2007) study of effective teaching; the *5 Dimensions of Teaching and Learning*, developed by the Center for Educational Leadership (www.k-12leadership.org); and the *STAR Protocol*, created by the BERC (Baker-Evaluation-Research-Consulting) Group (www.bercgroup.com). To find additional examples, just type "instructional frameworks" into your Internet search engine.

Professional Development Resources

Well-respected education leaders—including Richard Elmore, Arthur K. Ellis, Linda Darling-Hammond, Heidi Hayes Jacobs, Rick Stiggins, and Todd Whitaker—have investigated high-leverage teaching methods and shared what they have learned through articles, books, DVDs, online courses, webinars, YouTube videos, and presentations at major conferences. Since seeing these authors live is not always possible, there are print and audiovisual products available that are especially designed for onsite professional development.

Key Point

Before investing time, attention, and funds in *any* instructional resource, however, make sure you are comfortable with the foundational theories—you won't want a constructivist math program, for example, if your school district's philosophy favors a direct instruction approach. Next, test the efficacy of the education models, teaching materials, instructional frameworks, and professional development resources associated with the supporting theories. You do this by investigating pertinent applied research. This final step is critical.

Applied Research

Before theory moves into practice, it should be tested for its soundness; in the real world, sometimes even the best ideas don't pan out. Arthur K. Ellis helps educators understand this reality by describing the impact of various levels of research in his seminal book *Research on Educational Innovations* (2005). At the very first level, research takes place in "laboratory settings by psychologists, learning theorists, linguists, and others" (p. 30). It is from this research that promising theories are derived.

Experimental Studies

At the next level, research is "applied" by studying new theories and related practices in realistic settings—such as elementary and secondary classrooms—but under experimental conditions. These conditions usually include criteria upon which the participants are chosen for the study, pre- and post-testing, and control groups so that comparisons can be made between those who participate in the study and those who do not. From these experimental studies researchers get some idea about the effects that theories—and the practices and programs derived from them—will have in the real world.

Field Tests

The final research stage, if employed—amazingly, it is sometimes skipped—involves field-testing programs and materials arising from a given theory in settings *without* controlled conditions. Performance data is collected to see if the resources—and their underlying theories—meet expectations in authentic environments.

When I went hunting for a new reading program a while back, I conducted my own version of field-testing by visiting schools with similar profiles to mine that had experienced huge gains in reading. These schools had implemented a comprehensive, research-supported reading program with fidelity for several years. Although the reading program was demanding, the teachers in the schools I visited liked the instructional approach and were delighted with their students' progress. Needless to say, I was sold on the program.

Guiding Principles

My best advice to educators is to become well informed before making decisions that impact teaching and learning. To this end, here are the big ideas: before settling on *any* resource—education model, teaching materials, instructional frameworks, or professional development

---

Kelli Doherty
School Principal, Leavenworth, Washington

Degrees
B.A. Education
M. Ed. Curriculum and Instruction

Current Position
Principal, Icicle River Middle School

Previous Assignment
Principal, Osborne Elementary School

Osborne Elementary Awards
2010 Washington Achievement Award
2009 Great Schools Award
2008 School of Distinction Award
2004–2006 Academic Improvement Awards

Biggest Challenge
"Motivating teachers despite dwindling resources, staff cuts, and budget reductions coupled with a significant increase in job responsibilities and performance expectations. Educators are constantly required to do more with less."

Best Reward
"The best reward is walking down the hallways and seeing students who are happy, motivated to learn, and confident. I have tremendous pride in my staff, the relationships we build with students, and the gains students make each and every day."

approach—scrutinize the foundational theories, review the associated experimental studies, and ask about authentic field-testing. You are looking for evidence that the resource actually works in schools similar to your own. A word of caution: even dynamite resources will not be effective if poorly implemented or put into the hands of resistant teachers. Staff buy-in, ample training—at the start of the implementation process—and ongoing, sufficient resource materials (e.g., not *some* of the essential components but *all* of them), and close monitoring by instructional leaders underlie the success of any new approach.

Practitioners in Action

Let's say you've found the perfect research-driven resource—a powerful approach to teaching writing, a proven way to boost reading fluency, or a teacher-friendly instructional framework—and want to put it into practice. How do you go about it? You will pick up valuable tips from the talented educators in the Q & As that follow. Kelli Doherty is a highly effective middle-school principal whose previous school, Osborne Elementary, received multiple awards for improving student performance. Tim Bartlett is a secondary-school math coach who helps teachers drive up student achievement. Whatever your school's education level, you will find solid ideas in both interviews. Kelli and Tim have succeeded in helping teachers—including *good* teachers—become better teachers.

School Principal Q & A

Cathie: Good teachers are invaluable—what characteristics do you look for?

Kelli: Good teachers possess a wide range of characteristics that they draw from at different times. A good teacher essentially needs to be a mixed bag in order to adapt to the individual needs of students. For instance, a good teacher can nurture an emotionally fragile student but then turn around and provide clear structure and boundaries for another.

Cathie: Good teachers are also instructionally effective. What do you see them doing that sets them apart?

Kelli: Teachers must be "kid effective." These teachers are easy to spot. They are the ones you see out on the playground at recess and at sporting events. Instructionally, these teachers spend more time interacting with students than simply presenting information. They ask questions to pique curiosity and invite students

	to share and demonstrate what they have learned with others. My most effective teachers engage students in meaningful dialogue, adjust lesson content based on student feedback, provide opportunities for applied learning projects, and differentiate like crazy.
Cathie:	Sounds like you are after best-practice teaching. What does "best practice" mean to you?
Kelli:	Best practices are those that get results. They provide targeted knowledge and skills, maintain student interest, motivate children to learn, and meet the needs of a diverse population. For instance, what might be deemed best practice in a classroom full of native English speakers may be very different from what best practice looks like in a classroom with an English Language Learner population.
Cathie:	The kind of instructional practices you describe require teacher buy-in—how do you get it?
Kelli:	Nothing contributes to teacher buy-in more than shared decision-making. Before teachers buy into a new practice, they must believe in it and be convinced of its effectiveness. Teachers are among the most skeptical people I know. Most have been in the teaching profession for quite a while and they know what students will and will not respond to—they are too smart to fall for every new fad that comes our way. However, when teachers identify a need, they are very willing to find a solution. If teachers are part of the process of researching solutions—and find ones they think will work—they will sell it to their colleagues.
Cathie:	What advice do you have for school leaders striving to boost student achievement?
Kelli:	It's easy to get caught up in wanting to do everything better all at the same time! First, use data to target a subject for improvement. Next, look at what is getting in the way of your success. Is too much time being spent on discipline? How much time are teachers spending on this particular subject each day? Are teachers familiar with grade-level targets and what they mean? Also, which students are struggling? Boys? Girls? Low-income? It's important to be specific—then you can implement targeted interventions.
Cathie:	Sound advice from a principal whose leadership has garnered prestigious school awards—any other tips?
Kelli:	I also think it's important to take teachers to observe other schools that are successful in your area of deficit. Then collaborate as a team to implement a system that works for *your* school.

Kelli highlights school improvement essentials—put students first, be data-driven, drill down to essential goals, involve and empower teachers, and learn from the successes of others. In the next Q & A, Tim Bartlett shares strategies he has used successfully as both a teacher and an instructional coach.

Secondary-School Math Coach Q & A

Cathie: Improving student achievement is the end result of good instruction, and yet there are teachers at all levels who year after year fail to get results. How do you get these teachers to take a critical look at their own teaching?

Tim: I don't approach it at all from the standpoint of critiquing someone's instructional performance. It's not about that teacher or their ability, or me and my ability. I approach it from a "third point." This "third point" is a neutral point we can both look at without feeling guilty or laying blame. In this case, it's student learning. We focus our effort on that, and how to improve it. We pursue those things that might improve student learning: strengthening student engagement, gathering data from formative assessment and utilizing it effectively, drawing from the experiences and resources of colleagues, and reviewing literature on best practices. The process is *very* collaborative in nature, focusing on the shared concern of student learning—the third

---

Tim Bartlett
Secondary-School Math Coach

Degrees
B.A. Social Studies/English Education
M. Ed. Middle School Gifted Education

Current Assignment
Secondary Math Coach
Lake Stevens School District, Washington

Awards and Honors
2005 Student Leadership Award
2007 Washington State Math Coach Appointment
2008 Washington State Math Standards Revision Team Member

Biggest Challenge
"Finding funds and time for teachers to collaborate in meaningful ways is always a huge challenge."

Best Reward
"Being selected for the team that rewrote the Washington State math standards in 2008—I worked with some of the best math minds in our state and nation."

	point. I'm not a consultant bringing answers to an inadequate professional, but a partner in search of a solution.
Cathie:	You have helped a lot of teachers improve their performance. What are the keys to improving *student* performance?
Tim:	I think it's mainly about formative assessment and, even more specifically, the reaction to the data that has been gathered. It's about putting a name and a face with a problem, and then determining a plan for correcting the deficiency. Something like a chapter test or classroom-based assessment typically gives us some broad measures about how a group of students is performing, and how a student *within* that group is performing overall. But unless we dig a little deeper it may not tell us *who* doesn't know *what* and even more importantly *why*.
Cathie:	How do you get to the who, what, and why?
Tim:	In one district I helped teachers develop a series of quick assessments that were *very* specific to the state math standards and these assessments helped us answer those questions. In a way that's the easy part. The *hard* part is finding the time and personnel to correct the problem. There's no silver bullet. When dealing with RTI, every school has to determine its best course for providing the necessary interventions.
Cathie:	The response to intervention approach is foundational in improving teacher effectiveness. How does a school district support RTI efforts across schools?
Tim:	I think the district's responsibility is getting everyone on the same page, for example, making sure teachers realize state standards are *their* curriculum and drive instruction. Promoting the development of shared assessments based on the standards is also important—they provide a common ground for gauging the effectiveness of instruction and allow for collaborative discussions about how to improve student learning. Districts needn't take a heavy, top-down approach, but rather convey a clear understanding that these aspects are expectations. A system also needs to be established that verifies those things are happening. Most importantly, the district needs to provide the time for the professionals responsible for this work to do it. It can't be squeezed in before school in a half hour or after school with half of the people gone to coaching, club responsibilities, or other meetings.
Cathie:	You have been an exceptional secondary math teacher and now coach. Describe the elements that you believe characterize an ideal math lesson.
Tim:	I really don't think there's much difference between a good lesson in math and a good lesson in any other subject. It has little to do with a "traditional" versus an "integrated" approach

or with "whole-class/direct instruction" versus students working "inductively/deductively." Teachers just need a clear learning target that is communicated daily to their students in student-friendly language. Students also need to be engaged; for example, they should be able to articulate the learning goal for the lesson. A variety of instructional methods also helps to ensure student engagement across a wide scope of learning styles. Finally, the teacher and students should come away from the lesson with some clear indication of whether the goal has been met. That drives the next lesson.

Cathie: How about students—what's their role?

Tim: I like to see students involved in charting their own progress and making individual decisions about where they need more practice and help.

Cathie: Some teachers find it hard to make instructional changes. How do you get teachers to exchange ineffectual practices for improved ones?

Tim: The key is in focusing on student learning. Teachers want their students to be successful. When the focus is on that, it opens the door to discussions on how to improve it. As a math coach, once the teacher and I identify some things that might help, then it's my job to facilitate that change. I may do research for a teacher, help design some lessons, develop curriculum, find needed supplements or classroom supplies, and arrange for visitations to other classrooms or schools. I do whatever it takes to make it easy for that teacher to try something new and different.

Cathie: When you come across teachers who fail to take part in change endeavors, what do you do?

Tim: First of all, I would determine just how many teachers were choosing *not* to take part. It might be that we need to take another look at the goal and how it was determined; otherwise it would be an uphill battle from the start, destined for failure. But assuming that there's a core of teachers who feel strongly about the school improvement effort, I would let their enthusiasm and energy pull along those who are on the sidelines. It's impossible to force buy-in. People will simply make a token, superficial effort and wait for the new fad to pass. Growth in a school may start with a small nucleus of people. It isn't always the *number* of people who are involved at the start that determines the success or failure of the effort; it's the dedication of those who are involved that carry the effort along.

Cathie: Specifically, what can school leaders do to support the nucleus of teachers who step forward to embrace better practices?

Tim: Support and publicize their efforts. Little by little others start coming aboard. Informal talk in the hallways, around the copy

|||machine, and at lunch can focus attention on the improvement effort. Reminders or suggestions in the daily bulletin can keep the goal in front of people. Staff meetings provide a forum for highlighting accomplishments. Hopefully, most people want to become part of what's happening. A friend of mine once described it as "gentle pressure, relentlessly applied." I like that thought.

Cathie: What has been your most memorable success as a math coach?

Tim: At one middle school we did some really nice work with deep alignments, curriculum maps, and pacing guides, and I think ultimately it will pay off in the long run. But the thing I was most satisfied with was a decision we made to get rid of all basic math classes. We just felt that our "basic" kids were dropping further and further behind each year. We were trying our best, but instead of narrowing the gap it seemed to get wider. The students who were in basic math class only associated with other students who were struggling. The pace was slower and there were no positive peer role models who really liked math and were successful with it. Expectations were not high for this group. Even when we added a second math class that focused on improving basic skills, these students seemed to lag behind.

Cathie: Eliminating basic math was a huge step. How did you handle this?

Tim: Every student was enrolled in a regular grade-level math class. We also identified fifteen or twenty students who were most in need of help and designed a second math class around them. As a math department we agreed that two-thirds of the time in that class would be spent on preteaching the subject matter being covered in the regular class, such as vocabulary and skills. Teachers would literally teach the lesson ahead of time, but anticipate all the problems a student might have with the lesson. The remaining time was spent filling holes these students exhibited. When possible, we employed a computerized program to quickly identify those holes and provide individualized instruction and practice.

Cathie: You have certainly realized your mission as a math coach.

Tim: I don't like the title of math "coach" as it seems to carry with it the perception that one person has all the answers and runs the show. I see myself more as a facilitator for change. I don't necessarily determine the change needed, but rather help administrators and teachers identify it and then facilitate the steps needed in making the change.

Tim outlines vital steps in the complex process that leads to school change. It begins with building a collaborative, supportive partnership between school leaders and teachers. Orchestrating alignment comes next in regard to learning targets, formative assessments, and interventions. Students are in the forefront too, learning to track their achievement and identify the help they need to make gains. All the while, data is used to inform instruction and verify success. Although the change is slow, with leadership finesse and subtle pressure it takes hold, flourishes, and endures.

Best-Practice Strategies

Bringing best practice to teachers—and ultimately to life in classrooms—is an arduous journey requiring unflagging persistence and no end of patience. There are a multitude of steps involved and they rarely follow a linear pathway. There are pit stops, side roads, and the retracing of steps all along the way so that the trail to success resembles a Chutes and Ladders game more than a straight, upward line of trajectory. These realities, however, make the instructional leadership role stimulating, growth-provoking, and rewarding. Although these rewards seem far off at times, they *will* emerge when effective strategies are employed, such as the ones that follow.

Get Up to Speed

Enticing teachers to embrace best practices requires preparation that is in-depth and ongoing. Instructional leaders must know the research behind curriculum content, instructional delivery, academic screenings, and formative and summative assessments. They should also know the most effective ways to motivate students and to bring professional development to their teachers. In addition, school leaders should investigate how successful colleagues have implemented school improvement concepts and practices in their schools. Given the ambitious nature of the foregoing goals, how do you get up to speed? The job begins with lots of reading—professional books, magazines, journals, and websites. Although finding time to read is difficult, it is not insurmountable. The trick is to carve out time, every day, when you are free of distractions. I tackle professional reading early in the morning at home as I speed walk on my treadmill. In just thirty minutes I can wade through several articles or a hefty chapter from the latest education best seller (see Figures 4.2, page 68, and 4.3, page 69, for a professional reading plan and template). Listening to informative CDs as you drive to and from school helps, as does downloading

Figure 4.2 Cathie West's Professional Reading Plan

Books
- Marzano, R. (2010). *Formative assessment and standards-based grading.* Bloomington, IN: Solution Tree Press.
- McDonald, J. P., Mohr, N., Dichter, A., & McDonald, E. C. (2003). *The power of protocols: An educator's guide to better practice.* New York: Teachers College Press.
- Jacobs, J. E., & O'Gorman, K. L. (2012). *The learning leader: Reflecting, modeling, and sharing.* Larchmont, NY: Eye On Education.

National Publications
- *Educational Leadership*
- *PDK Kappan*
- *Principal*

State Publications
- *The Principal News*
- *Washington State Kappan*

Websites
- Association of Washington State Principals (http://awsp.org)
- National Association of Elementary School Principals (http://www.naesp.org)
- PDK International (http://pdkintl.org)
- ASCD (http://ascd.org)

Reading Associated with Professional Service
- Editorial Board, *Washington State Kappan*
- Communications Advisory Committee, Association of Washington State Principals
- Grant Selection Committee, PDK International

Research Associated with Professional Writing
- Draft a book about conflict management for Eye On Education.
- Write an article about principal stress reduction for AWSP's *Principal News*.
- Write an article about student leadership for NAESP's *Principal* magazine.

Figure 4.3 Professional Reading Template

Books

_____
_____
_____
_____

National Publications

_____
_____
_____
_____

State Publications

_____
_____
_____
_____

books to your favorite electronic device so that the time you spend waiting for meetings to start is put to good use. Other avenues to staying up to date include attendance at major conferences, such as the prestigious Assessment Training Institute (ati.pearson.com) which draws educators from across the globe; participation in webinars and online chat groups coordinated by professional associations, like ASCD and Phi Delta Kappa International; service on regional, state, and national committees; and professional writing. Drafting an article, book review, or book provides opportunities to expand your knowledge base due to the research and self-study that writing requires. Whatever direction you take, the overriding goal is to become the best best-practice resource for your teachers.

Figure 4.3 Professional Reading Template *(continued)*

Websites

_____
_____
_____
_____

Research Associated with Professional Service

_____
_____
_____
_____

Research Associated with Professional Writing

_____
_____
_____
_____

Teach Best Practice

Given the scarcity of education dollars, it has become tougher to immerse teachers in professional development. Funds for workshops, collaboration meetings, and substitute teachers who free teachers to visit other classrooms have all but dried up. What to do? Leading structured book studies is an approach that works exceptionally well (West, 2011b). By structured I mean providing reading guides, reflection questions, and application suggestions that draw teachers deeply into the chosen book's content.

Figure 4.4 Activity: Formative Assessment = Changes in Behaviors

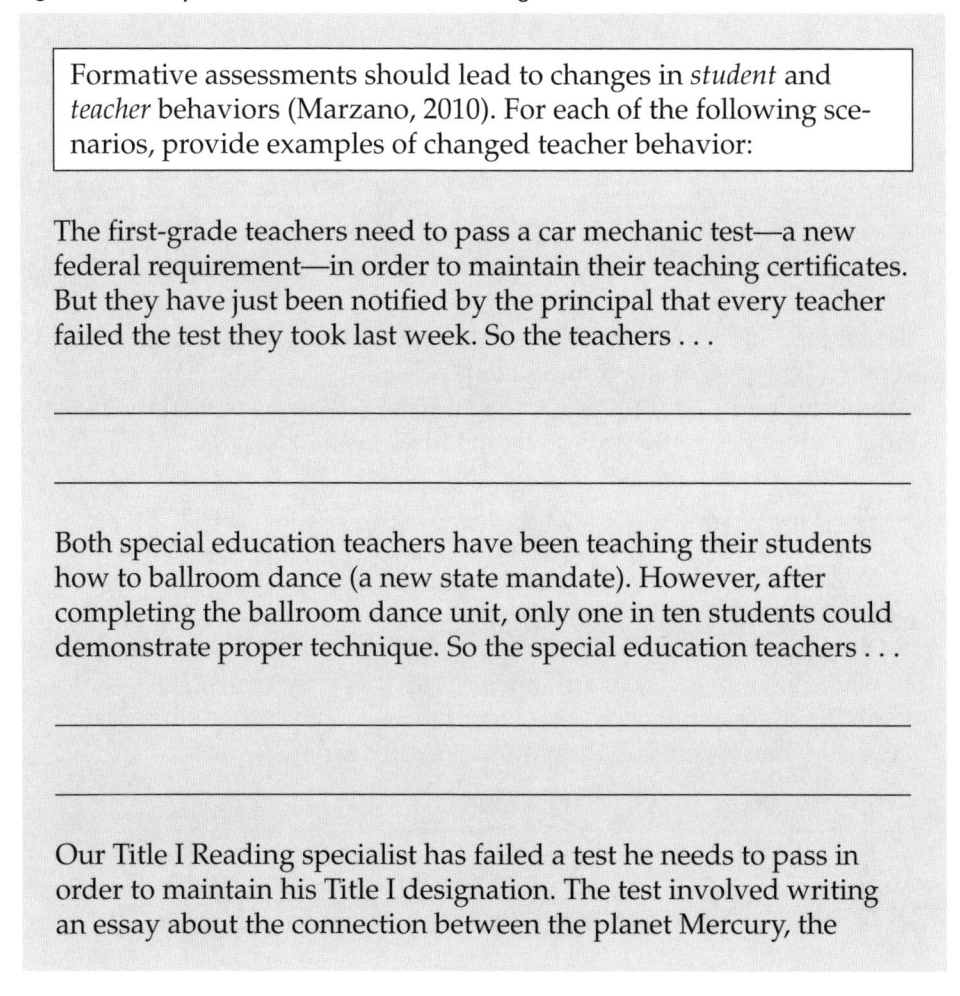

> Formative assessments should lead to changes in *student* and *teacher* behaviors (Marzano, 2010). For each of the following scenarios, provide examples of changed teacher behavior:

The first-grade teachers need to pass a car mechanic test—a new federal requirement—in order to maintain their teaching certificates. But they have just been notified by the principal that every teacher failed the test they took last week. So the teachers . . .

_____

_____

Both special education teachers have been teaching their students how to ballroom dance (a new state mandate). However, after completing the ballroom dance unit, only one in ten students could demonstrate proper technique. So the special education teachers . . .

_____

_____

Our Title I Reading specialist has failed a test he needs to pass in order to maintain his Title I designation. The test involved writing an essay about the connection between the planet Mercury, the

Another blue-ribbon idea is to turn teacher meetings into a classroom by presenting key ideas from powerful books about educational practice. I recently devoted twenty 30-minute staff meetings to the concepts and practices presented in *Formative Assessment and Standards-Based Grading* by Robert Marzano. I chose this book not only because I liked the author's approach to assessment, but because I suspected my teachers would find the book too demanding to navigate on their own. So I pulled "big ideas" from every chapter and created activities and discussion guides that would help teachers understand unfamiliar concepts and invite application in their classrooms. Figures 4.4 and 4.5 (page 73) provide examples of the materials I crafted.

Figure 4.4 Activity: Formative Assessment = Changes in Behaviors *(continued)*

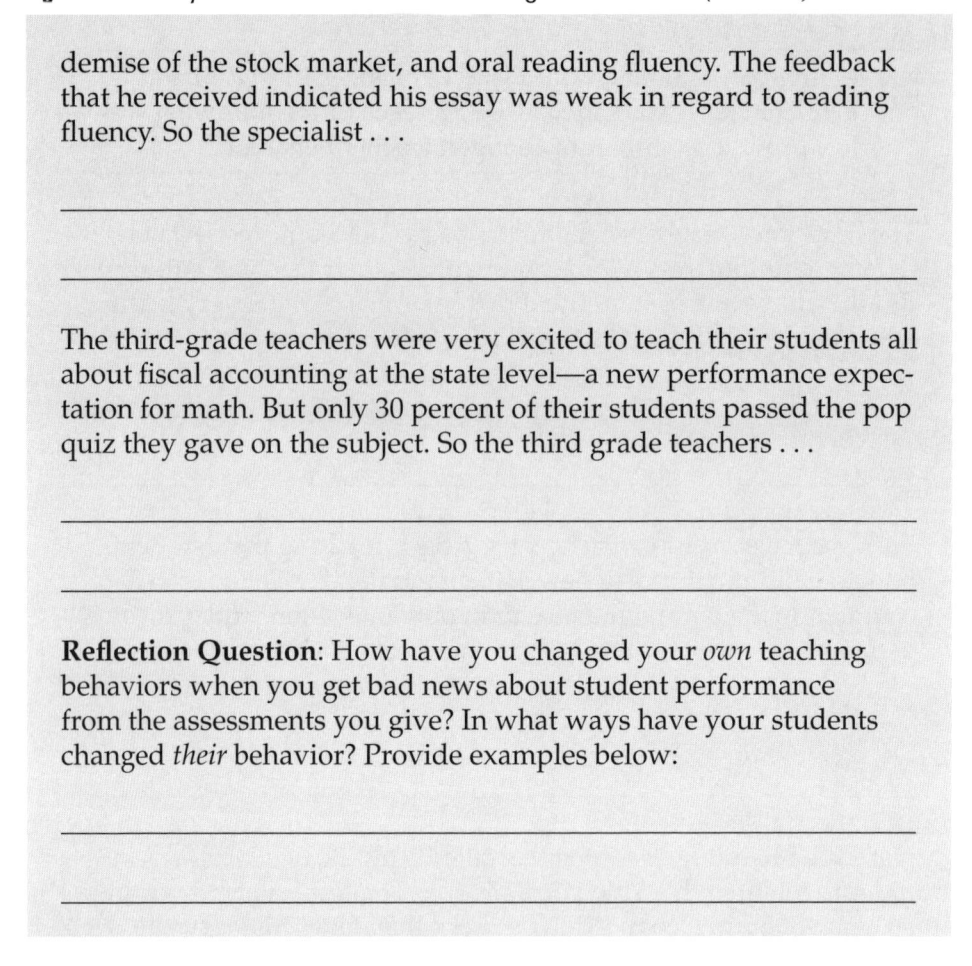

demise of the stock market, and oral reading fluency. The feedback that he received indicated his essay was weak in regard to reading fluency. So the specialist . . .

_____

_____

The third-grade teachers were very excited to teach their students all about fiscal accounting at the state level—a new performance expectation for math. But only 30 percent of their students passed the pop quiz they gave on the subject. So the third grade teachers . . .

_____

_____

Reflection Question: How have you changed your *own* teaching behaviors when you get bad news about student performance from the assessments you give? In what ways have your students changed *their* behavior? Provide examples below:

_____

_____

Identify Best-Practice Essentials

Tell your teachers in explicit terms what you have found—from reading, research, observation, and experience—to be essential to improving student learning. Here are my top ten essentials:

- Aligning instruction to adopted curriculum standards (McEwan, 2009)
- Sharing learning outcomes with students (Elmore, 2008)
- Teaching intentionally via explicit instruction (Ellis, 2005)
- Deepening student understanding through collaborative learning (Ellis, 2005)
- Honoring learning styles through differentiated instruction (Tomlinson, 2005)
- Correcting errors and reteaching (Guskey, 2010)

Figure 4.5 Activity: Formative Assessment Test Item Options

There are many types of formative assessment items, such as multiple-choice, matching, alternative-choice, true/false, multiple-response, fill-in-the-blank, and written-response (Marzano, 2010). Provide assessment examples for the items below:

Multiple-choice items provide a series of answers from which students are to select the correct one. Create a multiple-choice question for multiplying numbers with a calculator and provide four response choices:

_____

_____

_____

Matching items require students to match elements of information that are related. Typically more possible answers are offered than elements to which they are to be matched. Create lists of matching items for teaching supplies; include a few choices that are unrelated:

_____

_____

_____

- Scheduling ongoing practice opportunities (Marzano, 2003)
- Monitoring student progress through formative assessment (Marshall, 2008)
- Using data to evaluate and fine-tune instructional strategies (Copland & Knapp, 2006)
- Involving students in charting their own progress (Marzano, 2003)

Update your list periodically. A continual stream of fresh research about teaching effectiveness is becoming available in books, journals, and professional websites.

Figure 4.5 Activity: Formative Assessment Test Item Options *(continued)*

Alternative-choice items are like multiple-choice but offer only two possible answers. Create an alternative-choice item for a question about taking photos with a cell phone:

_____

_____

_____

True/false items require students to determine if a statement is accurate or inaccurate. Write three true/false items for a question about earning an advanced degree:

_____

_____

_____

Multiple-response items are like multiple-choice except that more than one of the alternatives can be correct. Write a multiple-response item for a question about teaching reading comprehension strategies (e.g., six responses with two being correct):

_____

_____

_____

_____

Figure 4.5 Activity: Formative Assessment Test Item Options *(continued)*

Fill-in-the-blank items require students to provide a response that fits into a specific phrase or sentence. Create a fill-in-the-blank sentence regarding preparation for state assessments:

_____

_____

_____

_____

Written-response items require students to write a correct answer to a question. Prepare a written response question regarding student motivation:

_____

_____

_____

_____

This exercise covered seven types of assessment items. Which do you typically use to assess your students? If not all seven, which do you plan to add to your assessment toolkit?

_____

_____

_____

_____

Adopt Core Instructional Materials

Over the decades the education pendulum has swung back and forth between core instructional programs—called "basals" not so long ago—that teachers are required to use and an eclectic, permissive approach that allows teachers to choose their own materials. I have experienced both ends of the spectrum and, given what I have learned, endorse core programs wholeheartedly. A well-selected core program is based on valid research and spirals from grade to grade, bringing continuity to learning targets, lesson design, and assessment practices. A comprehensive core program also provides a potpourri of supplemental resources that help teachers address the needs of diverse student populations, such as second language learners, special education students, and the highly capable. Core programs have additional advantages: students encounter familiar vocabulary, lesson procedures, and assessment formats; the work of teachers at one grade level supports the next; teachers can focus on improving instruction and supporting students instead of devoting precious time searching for or creating their own materials; and new teachers, instructionally weak veteran teachers, and substitutes have a solid teaching guide. Staff development is also focused and shared. As a bonus, the monetary investment in teaching materials is not wasted as teachers turn over. Replacement teachers are expected to use the core program—not request funds for something else.

Power-Up Programs

The best instructional programs capture the essence of required curriculum and present the most effective ways to deliver content to students. But putting an A+ program into the hands of teachers is just the first step. In order to realize the benefits, teachers need training regarding the new program's implementation, opportunities to deeply align required learning targets, and a review of the program's must-do components.

- Training: When new programs are introduced, teachers require an in-depth overview of the program's special features, teaching materials, instructional procedures, and assessment tools. Without initial—and ongoing—training, teachers may use a new program incorrectly, fail to use essential components, or default back to using the program that had been jettisoned.
- Deep alignment: A topic match between the new program and required learning targets is usually made by teachers, but that is just the first step. There also needs to be a match in cognitive complexity. This means an alignment between learning targets and what the program expects students to *know* and be able to *do*. For example, let's say there is a math target that expects first

graders to *explain* the attributes of a triangle. Does your new math program expect the same or do first graders only have to *recognize* triangles? If the program's spin on a learning target is less demanding, teachers will need to increase the complexity in order to fulfill curricular requirements.

- Must-do components: Instructional programs usually come with more features and materials than a teacher can reasonably use given available classroom time. So decisions have to be made regarding what to use and what to skip. For example, our reading program has three major components: (A) decoding and word analysis; (B) vocabulary development and comprehension; and (C) writing skills. We agreed that components A and B were essential parts of the day-to-day reading program but that C was optional. Be sure to identify must-do components in collaboration with your teachers.

Bring Frameworks to Life

If your school district has not yet adopted instructional frameworks—lead the charge. Frameworks provide unified expectations for exemplary teaching, a common language for discussing best practice, and a guide for professional development and teacher evaluation. Of course, selecting a framework is just the beginning in the instructional improvement process. You need to bring teaching frameworks to life by reviewing components at staff meetings, using frameworks for teacher observations, and giving feedback after classroom visits. We also use our frameworks when my teachers and I watch videos of exemplary teaching, set instructional improvement goals, or tour classrooms to watch teaching in action.

See to Believe

Successful teachers are the most powerful change agents—their instructional acumen carries weight with peers because they too work in the trenches, encountering the same kinds of teaching challenges, whether it be subduing a recalcitrant student or putting across a difficult curricular concept. You can tap into this credible resource by scheduling classroom visitations—we call them "learning walks"—with your teachers. Take grade-level teams to visit highly effective teachers, such as teachers at the grade level below and above. For example, a fourth-grade team could visit three or more successful teachers in grades three and five. It also works to have intermediate teachers visit primary classrooms and K–3 teachers visit upper-grade rooms. Just make sure you structure the visits by providing an observation guide, such as your school's instructional frameworks; setting constructive parameters, such as looking for positives—not faults; and debriefing after each visit.

Be the Best Model

If you expect your teachers to use best practices, then you had better do so too. Staff meetings—which should have an instructional focus—provide a prime opportunity. Tell teachers the purpose of the meeting and what they will gain from it, such as learning a new teaching or assessment technique, and liven up presentations with stories, examples, visual aids, research tidbits, and activities. Review Key 2 for additional information about ways to model good teaching and more effectively engage teachers.

Put Students in the Spotlight

What if the accountability movement came to a screeching halt? What if student achievement mandates at all levels were abruptly abandoned? Would zeroing in on best practice still matter? There is obviously only one answer to this rhetorical question—an emphatic "yes." Best practice matters because we want the *best* for our students. But you cannot assume that all teachers share the same urgency to improve student performance. Some staff members may still long for the good old days when teaching school was a low-profile profession far from the public spotlight. So remind teachers every chance you get that students *are* and *will* remain the prime motivation for our work.

Praise Progress

Don't forget to tell teachers you value their utilization of best practices, even in the early stages when implementation has not yet been perfected. For example, you might notice a teacher struggling with a workshop format in an attempt to differentiate instruction. Be sure to praise this effort—specifically noting what went well—with a handwritten note that you drop on the teacher's desk as you depart or by sending an on-the-spot e-mail via your electronic note pad. Over time, your specific praise will make the teacher's practice perfect.

Wrap-Up: Zero In on Best Practice

Key Concepts

- Best practices get results—students learn.
- Good teachers demonstrate a student-centered approach to teaching, plan well-designed lessons and learning activities, use research-based instructional techniques, and assess student learning skillfully.

- Learning theories of varying reliability provide the foundation for education models, teaching materials, instructional frameworks, and professional development resources.
- Before choosing any resource, investigate the program's foundational theories, experimental studies, and field-testing in authentic settings.
- New instructional programs require staff buy-in, ample training and resources, and ongoing guidance from instructional leaders.
- Savvy school leaders and teachers not only stay current but also learn from the successes of others.
- Improving student achievement is a collaborative process that involves eliciting teacher support, engaging students in the learning process, utilizing effective teaching and assessment practices, and using data to verify success.

Best Strategies

- Stay professionally up to date through reading, in-service, committee work, and writing.
- Give teachers the training they need to implement new programs successfully.
- Identify high-leverage teaching practices and share them with your staff.
- Adopt research-supported and curriculum-aligned core instructional materials.
- Strengthen instructional programs through training, deep alignment, and identification of nonnegotiable teaching components.
- Bring frameworks to life through teacher-principal learning walks.
- Model best practices as you lead staff and curriculum meetings.
- Provide teachers ample and specific praise for their efforts to refine their teaching.
- Keep students in the forefront.

Steps to Success

- Choose a core instructional program that your school is using and investigate its foundational theories, experimental studies, and any field-testing that occurred during its development. Is the program instructionally sound? Why or why not?
- What are the teaching practices that you believe to be critical? Make a list, including the research behind them. Share these practices—and the research—with your staff.

5

Tap into Teacher Leaders

> Being a strategic talent manager requires not only acquiring and developing staff, but also creating the working conditions in which staff fully commit their time and energy.
>
> —Steven M. Kimball

Leadership has been under the social science microscope for multiple decades—I have sifted through research and commentary going back to the 1920s—but, given the complexity of the concept, experts have yet to agree on a definition (Ogawa, 2005). So I am on pretty safe ground to put my own spin on this elusive concept. Here's my interpretation: A leader is someone people want to follow. If you agree with this elliptic take on leadership, you will appreciate this cautionary note: Be careful whom you put into a leadership role.

"School leader" is a descriptor generally associated with the principal, whose success rests upon the degree to which he or she manifests the following qualities: the leader is visionary, highly motivated, ethical, knowledgeable, organizationally skilled, collaborative, and people-sensitive (CCSSO, 2008). Most educators would agree with these sterling traits, but what do they look like in action? Proficient school leaders—the persons whom people most *want* to follow—gain the trust and confidence of teachers by what they *do*. They set high standards and clear priorities, run efficient schools, distribute resources equitably, know their people and their programs, and recognize good work and hard jobs. All these functions are essential, but principals are not superheroes—they need help. Here is where teacher leaders—if thoughtfully *selected*, *prepared*, and *coached*—step in.

Teacher Leaders

It is well accepted among educators that "teachers" are defined by the effectiveness of their instructional outcomes. In other words, when students learn, we've got teachers; and when students don't learn, we have something else—perhaps nothing more than a cadre of well-meaning presenters. This teaching-learning link is applicable to teacher leaders: when these superstars roll into action, people learn.

True teacher leaders are not as easy to spot as you might think. There are many teachers who step into the school spotlight by taking on extra jobs; they become club advisers, practicum teachers, committee members, and new teacher mentors. These valuable volunteers, however, may or may not become a major force in their schools. Teacher leaders, on the other hand, play *leading* roles by coordinating grade-level or department activities, assisting their principals with administrative and instructional responsibilities, and directing major projects. Over time, teacher leaders become highly influential; when they work in tandem with their principals, the school transformation potential is infinite.

Select

Given the power of teacher leadership, principals should not approach its development passively. Teacher leaders should be actively recruited. This process begins by establishing links to teachers who are already playing supportive roles. These are the dedicated souls who serve on—but don't lead—advisory councils, student services committees, curriculum development teams, and the like. It is from these ranks that principals usually find teachers willing to step into leadership positions, such as department heads, committee chairs, project coordinators, teachers on special assignments (TOSAs), and administrative interns.

Thought and care should underlie teacher leader recruitment. First and foremost, these teachers must be highly effective with students so that their credibility with peers is solid. They should also be in sync with their principal's approach to strengthening teacher and student performance, undaunted by challenges, and passionate about their profession. My most dependable recruits have, in addition, been fast learners, sensitive communicators, and adept problem-solvers.

Prepare

Few teachers complete coursework devoted solely to leadership, so recruits need their principals to provide experiences that broaden their knowledge base. I take teachers to the same trainings I participate in, such as management workshops, school administrator conferences, and leadership seminars. For example, I recently attended the National Association of Elementary School Principals' annual conference with my TOSA and four high-powered teacher leaders. I also appointed two teachers to our school district's Washington State Leadership Academy Team and found grant money to send lead teachers to a summer literacy conference. Opportunities like these empower teachers by strengthening their confidence and building foundational leadership knowledge and skills.

Strong direction and modeling are also imperative. When you assign projects, for example, prepare teacher leaders for success by outlining their specific responsibilities, suggesting steps for completing pertinent tasks, and specifying desired outcomes. If there are products to be produced, model development steps or provide samples to consider as a starting point. The overriding principle is never to assume that teacher leaders—no matter how bright or enthusiastic—know what *you* know.

Coach

When you see the word "mentor," think of a guide, but when you see "coach," picture a trainer (*Merriam-Webster's Collegiate Dictionary*, 2008). The guidance provided by mentors is usually low-key, nondirective, and comes in the form of modeling or suggestions. A coach, on the other hand, provides explicit training that includes step-by-step directions and instructive feedback. Teacher leaders benefit from both approaches but gain knowledge and skills more quickly—and make fewer mistakes—when coached. For example, should you ask a teacher leader to head a difficult committee, such as creating a new report card, don't simply hand over copies of the current cards and wait for results. Take time to explain in detail how to handle this kind of assignment effectively. Talk about the importance of selecting committee members with varied educational backgrounds and experiences, creating meeting norms, setting clear goals and realistic timelines, conducting in-depth research, and coordinating with administrators and special programs. As the committee work unfolds, attend meetings so that you can affirm effective leadership practices like listening and paraphrasing or keeping committee members on topic. Give postmeeting pointers too, such as how to control the use of limited time or bring a divided committee to consensus. Intentional coaching will ensure that the leadership tasks teachers take on are productive and rewarding. The following Q & As highlight the role of teacher leaders.

Practitioners in Action

The word "strategy" pertains to the tactics one employs to reach an objective. Kimball informs us that "a school's teaching talent becomes *strategic* when it's systematically linked to school instruction-improvement strategies, to the competencies needed to enact the strategies, and to success in boosting student learning" (2011, p. 13, italics mine). The strategic use of teacher leaders, for example, will push a school closer to its goals.

I interviewed a highly regarded teacher, Valerie Anderson, to learn about her own leadership development. I also arranged for a group of successful teacher leaders to talk about their roles with Lois Frank, the impressive school district consultant highlighted in Key 1. The interviews shed light on how talented teachers become *strategic* teachers.

Lead Teacher Q & A

Teacher leaders are a unique breed. They willingly assume leadership responsibilities without compensation but with all the associated risks—failed projects, unpopular decisions, and boatloads of problems. Who are these special teachers and what motivates them? Valerie Anderson, a veteran fifth-grade teacher, broadens our understanding:

Cathie: You are highly thought of as a teacher leader in your school district—not just by administrators but by your colleagues. How did that come about?

Valerie: It seems strange that people view me as a "teacher leader." Helping others do their best for every student is part of my job.

Cathie: And you do that job exceptionally well; in fact, you have become the go-to person for the teachers in your school. Why do you think teachers seek you out?

Valerie: My life experiences—coming to teaching later in life—gave me the understanding that all of us have different strengths and different points of view. I also understand what teachers need in the way of time, materials, and support. I was blessed in my practicum experiences with diverse placements with many different types of teachers. Some of them were very helpful in a nonthreatening way but others were *not* so helpful. These experiences gave me valuable reference points; they shaped my perspective on leading other teachers.

Cathie: Taking the lead is not always comfortable. What needs to be in place before a teacher assumes this kind of risk?

Valerie: You have to have a supportive culture in your building for teacher leaders to flourish and grow. A culture that divides and isolates makes it safer for teachers to withdraw and not step out

> **Valerie Anderson**
> *Fifth-Grade Teacher, Mountain Way Elementary School*
>
> **Degrees**
> B.Ed. Western Washington University
> M.Ed. Reading and Literacy, City University of Seattle
>
> **Current Assignments**
> Fifth-Grade Teacher
> Grade-Level Team Leader
> Principal Advisory Council
>
> **Awards and Honors**
> 1999–2000 Lake Stevens School District Volunteer of the Year
> 2005 Snohomish County Public Utility District Energy Grant for Water Rockets
> 2008 Sylvan Learning Teachers Who Make a Difference Award
> 2009 Intermec Science Grant Recipient
> 2009 Laser Science Training Participant
> 2010 Summer Institute of Life Science Participant
> Washington State Leadership Academy Teacher Representative
>
> **Biggest Challenge**
> "Meeting the needs of *all* my students."
>
> **Best Reward**
> "Students taking responsibility for their own learning."

as leaders. I have been very fortunate to work in a building that nurtures teacher leaders.

Cathie: What experiences prepared you for a leadership role?

Valerie: My mom was a great influence on my life. Her attitude was that if something needs doing, you just step up and do it. I was also placed in leadership roles through programs like ASB [Associated Student Body] in high school, 4-H, and FFA [Future Farmers of America]—even when I didn't think I had the required knowledge or skills! But I was able to learn from these experiences.

Cathie: How about professionally?

Valerie: I can't single out just one experience. Attending a week-long science in-service that prepared teachers to become teacher trainers boosted my confidence. And I organized Young Authors activities that brought authors to district elementary schools. That was a real leadership learning experience. It was also seeing what my formal and informal mentors have done, seeing the benefits for students and staff, and wanting to help.

Cathie: Tell me your thoughts about mentoring and the people who supported you.

Valerie: A mentor supports my efforts in improving my craft as a teacher. My formal mentors were my practicum supervisor and new teacher adviser, but my informal mentors include principals, teachers at all levels, and specialists. Some of these people probably don't even know I consider them mentors. I am just really good at finding strong people to learn from and share with.

Cathie: Teacher leadership work is demanding, time-consuming, and at times frustrating. What is the payoff?

Valerie: The payoff is the same as watching students when the light comes on and learning takes place. When teachers come back and tell me they tried something new, applied what they learned or heard, it honestly feeds my ego. I know I made a difference. This gives me the reserves to support the teacher who is more challenging, needs additional help, or has a different modality for learning. Just like with students, I appreciate knowing that I am doing a good job and making progress.

Cathie: Sounds like "making a difference" is the biggest reward.

Valerie: I work with children—and teachers—to make a difference, to help them have better lives and more opportunities. Positive feedback builds my resilience and keeps me going.

Valerie zeros in on experiences that helped her grow as a leader. Mentoring by teachers and administrators—both formal and informal—were huge influences. A supportive school culture coupled with specialized training came next. Throughout, Valerie's own desire to serve was the driving force that led to her biggest reward: "making a difference."

Teacher Leaders Q & A

The following Q & A with Lois Frank puts the spotlight on school culture and how it shapes teacher leadership. Interview participants include Valerie Anderson along with Cheryl Larsen, teacher on special assignment; Tami Liebetrau, second-grade teacher; Linda Johnson, reading and math specialist; and Robyn Ross, first-grade teacher.

Lois: Student achievement has steadily improved in your school. Why do you think that has happened?

Cheryl: There's a culture of improvement—an unwavering focus on student achievement and our *own* improvement. Professionalism is infectious—teachers want to do better. We've looked at painful data and learned how to move on.

Valerie: There has been a concentrated effort to improve learning for all students. There has been focused leadership on helping teachers

	improve. The leadership has vision and a belief that is transmitted to all staff. The principal welcomes new staff, telling them they can make a difference—their talents and leadership are encouraged.
Linda:	We have strong leadership here. We learn about research and best practices, look at assessments and data, and reflect on what has worked and not worked. We are focused and intentional.
Lois:	How about culture and collaboration?
Linda:	There is a climate of working together so we can better ourselves. It is not a building where there is competition.
Tami:	The environment is positive. We are a close staff—helping each other. We get the work done and have fun doing it. Kids feel safe because they see teachers working without tension.
Valerie:	We share our challenges and talk about student achievement in open ways so that we can find out who in our building can help us if we are stuck. Collaboration ends the isolation that stagnates some teachers.
Lois:	Any other big ideas?
Robyn:	Everyone's opinions and thoughts are valued. We have staff meetings with conversations about work and grade level and cross-grade-level collaboration. The environment is relaxed but purposeful. We don't waste our minutes.
Valerie:	School is not something that is done *to* you. You have to participate—staff and students are *not* passive.

(West & Frank, 2010, pp. 19–20)

These teachers describe an environment where teachers are highly engaged in the change process, the work is collaborative, leadership is shared and respected, and the mission—improving student performance—is strong. Their school is a dynamic place where teacher leaders thrive.

Teacher Leader Development Strategies

Key 5 has covered a variety of ways to nurture teacher leadership: creating a supportive culture, recruiting viable candidates, providing adequate preparation, and being a "guide on the side" through intentional coaching. Here are some additional strategies for your leadership development toolkit:

Assign Strategic Tasks

Teacher leaders willingly pick up extra responsibilities, such as spearheading food drives, supervising student safety patrols, and planning staff talent shows. As necessary as these events are, they are generally not tied to school goals so they will seldom help a school's improvement process move forward. So as much as is possible, align the work of teacher leaders to school initiatives. When my school began implementing the Common Core State Standards, for example, I sent four lead teachers to trainings that would prepare them to support colleagues during the transition process. They helped me lead the first orientation session and quickly became the gurus for "Common Core" throughout the building. I used the same tactic to expand teachers' use of formative assessments. After I had presented ten hours of assessment "big ideas" to my faculty—via a series of jam-packed staff meetings—I arranged for several influential teachers to attend an assessment institute. The teachers returned to school excited that the assessment concepts we had explored at the faculty meetings had been addressed in greater depth at the institute. The teachers had also picked up additional assessment ideas that they eagerly shared with colleagues. The enthusiasm of these teacher leaders propelled the concept of formative assessment forward, making them strategic players in the school improvement process.

Model

Most of the teacher leaders I have worked with have not completed administrative coursework or practicums. So modeling leadership—*what* to do and *how* and *when*—was critical. Novice leaders learn from watching their principals in action at curriculum work sessions, in-services, faculty meetings, book studies, goal conferences, and the like. This modeling—coupled with coaching—equips teachers to handle the difficulties that come with leadership, such as time constraints, inflexible staff members, and too many demands. When it comes to complexities like these, your coaching should include "metacognitive processing aloud." This means you don't just model, you share your thinking as well. Tell your teacher leaders *why* you are taking a slow approach to a major change, for example, or surveying staff before making a controversial decision. I treat my teacher leaders a lot like administrative interns, which better prepares them for taking the lead.

Welcome Different Viewpoints

As you increase communication with teacher leaders, expect to hear views that are at odds with your own. Lead teachers might have different goals in mind for the school or advocate an approach to driving up achievement that you find questionable. In *Reframing Teacher Leadership to Improve Your School*, Reeves points out that diverse perspectives bring opportunities (2008). In the case of teacher leaders, differences of opinion invite deeper discussions about pedagogy and investigative activities, such as action research, field-testing, and evidence-gathering. Although disconcerting at times, varied views are valuable when we learn from them. Ultimately, school leaders and lead teachers will need to get on the same page. This may take time, but the steps it takes to get there will be as professionally rewarding as the final outcome.

Mobilize

When you have problems to fix, mobilize the troops—put your most effective lead teachers into action. For example, a few years back I had several teachers unexpectedly reassigned to my school due to reduction in force measures. There were teachers from secondary schools who were baffled by our complex reading program and teachers with elementary backgrounds whose knowledge of the program was at the emergent level. Not surprisingly, the biggest hurdle for all of these teachers was decoding—letter sounds, sound-letter correspondence, and blending. I drafted my strongest primary reading teacher to individually review these skills with the new teachers. This was soon followed by whole-faculty presentations and teacher observations when it became apparent that every teacher in the school needed a decoding brush-up. This experience reinforced my belief that deploying lead teachers when problems emerge provides quick solutions to unexpected problems.

Support

As for any professional, the effectiveness of teacher leaders can be enhanced by access to time and funds. Teacher leaders need time to collaborate with their principals, assist peers, research innovative practices, prepare for faculty presentations, and write grants for special projects. Extra funds may not only subsidize needed time—buying subs or paying for extended hours—but bring needed supplies, specialized trainings, and books and multimedia resources from education publishers. Supporting lead teachers with time and money—not just grants but also building budget dollars—should be a given.

Lead teachers also require their school leader's support when engaged in professional studies, such as attaining national board certification, a master's degree, or certification endorsements. Be prepared to loan out professional books and journals for research, share information from websites you subscribe to, and permit teacher leaders to leave school early for classes. Providing support may seem burdensome at times, but the more lead teachers grow, the more they give back.

Encourage Risk-Taking

In *Teacher Leadership That Strengthens Professional Practice*, Danielson reminds administrators that it takes courage to be a lead teacher because "at times, teacher leaders must go out on a limb; success is not always guaranteed" (2006, p. 38). For me, Danielson's observation called to mind a bright, enthusiastic principal intern who took on the revitalization of her school's discipline program, a tricky endeavor for the most experienced administrator. The intern's preparation—research, formation of an advisory team, and plans for committee work sessions—was solid. Nevertheless, all the usual bugs that accompany change came out of the woodwork. Team members argued about behavior expectations, engaged in aimless discussions about the appropriateness of various student incentives, and obsessed over trivial matters, such as the cover design for the new student behavior guide. Sometimes team meetings just did not go well. Throughout the trying process, however, the school's principal became the intern's best resource. Eventually every difficulty was resolved and the discipline program revision completed. Equally rewarding for the principal was learning that the intern credited the success of the project to the principal's unfailing confidence and support.

Highlight Results

There is nothing more motivating than being publicly recognized for your work. So look for ways to acknowledge the accomplishments of teacher leaders by highlighting their activities in school board reports, staff bulletins, community press releases, and parent newsletters. Featuring lead teachers' successes in professional articles and books provides additional ways to praise achievements.

State and national award nominations are also valued by teachers, not only for the recognition but for the stipends these kinds of awards usually bestow for professional development. Never assume that winning a prestigious honor is impossible. Over the years my teacher leaders have earned Christa McAuliffe and Milken Educator awards as well as Teacher of the Year recognition at the state and national levels. Granted, tributes like these require considerable work—the application processes are formidable—but honoring deserving teachers is definitely worth the effort.

Provide Incentives

Although teacher leaders absorb responsibilities without incentives in mind, they will appreciate tangible recognition. The tangibles include "good news" notes, certificates honoring their accomplishments, time-off tickets that allow them to flex their schedules, and letters of recommendation for new positions. Project stipends that compensate teachers monetarily for time worked beyond the school day are also highly prized. Using grant funds, I was able to put a teacher to work—after contract hours—coordinating our Highly Capable Learner Program. Another teacher was given a similar stipend for overseeing my school's state and district assessment activities. Pay for extra work puts more than dollars in teachers' pockets: remuneration affirms the valuable role teacher leaders play in high-performing schools. Teachers who take on extra projects are gold—don't take them for granted.

Wrap-Up: Tap into Teacher Leaders

Key Concepts

- Discerning school leaders are thoughtful about whom they put into leadership roles.
- Proficient principals gain the trust and confidence of their teachers by what they *do*.
- When teacher leaders roll into action, people learn.
- The school transformation potential is infinite when teacher leaders work in tandem with their principals.
- When recruiting teacher leaders, principals should look for highly skilled educators who are passionate about their profession.
- Principals should actively broaden teachers' leadership knowledge base and skills.
- Teacher leaders are more successful when responsibilities, project implementation steps, and assignment objectives are clearly delineated.
- Leadership recruits require intentional, explicit coaching that includes direct instruction and corrective feedback.
- The strategic use of teacher leaders will push a school closer to its goals.

Best Strategies

- Be strategic—tie the work of teacher leaders to specific school goals.
- Transfer leadership knowledge and skills to teacher leaders through modeling and explaining what you do and how.
- Keep in mind that different perspectives bring opportunities for professional growth.
- Mobilize the troops when you have problems to solve—put your most effective lead teachers into action.
- Enhance the effectiveness of teacher leaders by providing extra time, funds, and professional development.
- Be a guide on the side when teacher leaders take on challenging assignments.

- Look for ways to recognize lead teachers by featuring their accomplishments in written communications; presentations at school, district, and state meetings; and through award nominations.
- Provide teacher leaders with tangible rewards for assuming extra assignments.

Steps to Success

- Who are your teacher leaders and how do you sustain their interest? What motivates them? Which projects do they prefer? Take time to interview your lead teachers one by one to learn more about their views, interests, and motivations. This will help you utilize their talents more effectively.
- How can you use teacher leaders more strategically? Take a thoughtful look at your school and district goals and then generate a list of projects that lead teachers can take on to support goal attainment. Don't forget to solicit ideas from your lead teachers as well.

6

Confront Change Challengers

> If teachers are sabotaging new initiatives, leaders must have the moral courage to confront the teachers, clearly articulate the expectations, jointly set benchmarks for improvements . . . and monitor progress.
> —Dr. Gene Sharratt

Universal popularity is not a realistic goal for principals. When teachers violate rules, policies, and procedures, these regrettable incidents must be addressed by school leaders. Over the years I have confronted teachers about a variety of startling misdeeds—floating fish skeletons in neglected classroom tanks, potentially dangerous bat houses hung above playgrounds, death-threatening peanuts fed to allergic kindergarteners, and unruly boys flicked with flyswatters. I was not beloved by these errant teachers—or their union reps—but doing my job was not a mandate I took lightly. I comfort myself knowing that other principals would have done the same; determinedly bringing policy blunders, safety snafus, and demeaning discipline to the attention of unthinking teachers. Paradoxically, I also know that among these conscientious administrators are principals who tolerate teachers who fail to support school change efforts. Why would a school leader ignore such an important issue? Perhaps it's because teacher "change challengers" wear a perplexing variety of disguises.

The Change Challengers

Teachers who fail to embrace reform measures may go unnoticed at first, and this is unfortunate. The earlier teacher resistance is addressed, the faster the turnaround. Before taking action, however, it helps to know the type of change challenger you are dealing with. Here are the ones you will most frequently encounter:

The Confused

Teachers want to do right by the students they serve—and by their profession—but despite this zeal some may fail to successfully engage in school renewal efforts. It's not that these dedicated souls aren't trying; they are simply baffled by the lofty yet ill-defined goals of the reform movement. There might be an expectation, for example, that teachers honor a diverse student population by developing a "culturally rich and relevant school climate." The rhetoric is attractive, but teachers may be left wondering what "climate" and "rich and relevant" mean exactly, how to translate these terms into classroom practice, and what steps to take to attain desired outcomes. School renewal confusion becomes evident when teachers are unable to articulate their school's mission, explain how to carry out project objectives, or formulate pertinent professional goals.

The Distracted

School improvement efforts fail to register with some teachers because they are distracted. A baby is coming, a husband has lost his job, a child is seriously ill, or a divorce is looming. I once asked a teacher why he was professionally coasting after years of dedicated service; he admitted that he and his wife were on the verge of financial collapse. This teacher was so worried about losing the family home that he had no energy left for anything else. In addition to financial concerns, there are a myriad of other distractions that compete for teachers' attention, like coaching ball teams, appearing in community theater productions, and running for public office. Job sharing is also diverting as teachers try to juggle family responsibilities—like brand-new babies—with demands in the classroom. One teacher candidly disclosed, after several years of part-time work, "When it came to school, I mentally checked out." Clues that you are dealing with distracted teachers include declining student performance; late submissions of required reports; limited participation in professional meetings; and poor-quality products, such as lesson handouts riddled with typos, student progress reports with unsubstantiated grades, and teacher web pages that have become cobweb sites.

The Discouraged

Some teachers put forth their best effort but can't seem to pull it together instructionally—their students' performance scores are stagnant or, worse, declining. The discouraged include rookie teachers with emerging skills; experienced teachers new to grade levels or course assignments; and well-intentioned teachers whose competency levels are marginal. The indicators for discouraged teachers include weak student test scores, little or no enthusiasm for new school endeavors, unambitious professional goals, and a lack of confidence in the capacity of students to improve. Sadly, discouraged teachers lose their motivation over time, are reluctant to take risks, and see any change effort as just one more opportunity for failure.

The Anxious

I once worked for a superintendent whose ruthless approach to improving student test scores precipitated high anxiety among the district's instructional staff. Teachers dreaded their state's annual release of test results and cringed at the thought of the performance reviews that would follow should scores fail to improve. According to Goleman, when anxiety is out of whack, "we plunge into what neuroscientists call 'cognitive dysfunction'" (2006, p. 268). We don't concentrate, think, or perform at our best. An overanxious workforce worries excessively, feels overwhelmed, and experiences fear about measuring up. Not surprisingly, overanxious teachers perform marginally or jump ship at the first opportunity—moving to nontested classrooms within their school or out of the school district entirely. High anxiety sucks the life out of an organization by shifting teachers' energy from school improvement to self-protection.

The Coasters

There is a leadership quip that goes something like this: "In any organization, there are only a handful of people holding it together—everyone else is just posing." Fortunately there are few teacher/posers in schools, but the ones that *do* exist do the bare minimum to get by instructionally, enthusiastically embrace potlucks and birthday celebrations but complain when curriculum meetings are scheduled, and decline the chance to help with challenging work, like aligning textbooks with new standards or crafting new report cards. The coasters seem professionally misplaced; one is left wondering why they chose education as a career.

The I-Centered

The teacher who falls into the I-centered category never sees the proverbial forest, just his or her tree. Making changes that benefit students and the school organization as a whole is not within this teacher's frame of reference. I-centered teachers ignore evidence that contradicts their way of thinking, professional development that questions their professional practice, and opportunities to collaborate with peers. Because I-centered teachers insist that their way of doing things is the best way, their support for new practices is in the near-to-nonexistent range.

The Saboteurs

Although saboteurs are in the minority, no list of change challengers is complete without them. Unless suppressed, these "educators" cast a pall upon the entire process of upgrading student and staff performance. The saboteurs include the holdouts, who are issued a brand-new writing program but continue to use the previous one; the cynics, who seem to enjoy casting doubts on the probable success of *any* endeavor, from increasing parents' attendance at conferences to improving the quality of students' homework; the naysayers, who openly object to any demanding proposals, such as implementing a hands-on science approach or establishing professional learning communities; and the whiners, for whom everything is *too* complicated, *too* time-consuming, and *too* much work. Like the coasters, these staff members appear to have stumbled into the wrong profession.

Key Points

Teacher avoidance of change comes in a multiplicity of forms. Some teachers may be confused about the role they play while others are too distracted to move beyond the classroom survival mode. Emotions also come into play when teachers become discouraged or overly anxious due to heightened expectations. And then there are the teachers who are not working up to their potential or have become too focused on their *own* interests at the expense of students and their schools. Saboteurs are out there too—out of sync, self-absorbed educators who actively undermine their school's improvement efforts. Change challengers are a huge stumbling block—they are not to be ignored.

Practitioners in Action

How should school leaders approach teachers who avoid change? I asked Dr. Gene Sharratt for his take on teacher resistance and school leadership responsibilities. Gene is an ideal leadership resource: he directs Washington State University's Superintendent Certification Program and the Washington Association of School Principals' Evaluation Leadership Framework Project. His insights are priceless.

Dr. Gene Sharratt
Clinical Associate Professor, Washington State University

Degrees
Ph.D. Curriculum and Instruction
M.A. Guidance and Counseling
B.A. Education

Current Projects
Director, Washington State University Superintendent Certification Program
Project Manager, Washington Association of School Principals Evaluation Leadership Framework

Awards and Honors
National Educational Administrator of the Year
Washington State Superintendent of the Year
Washingtonian of the Year

Biggest Challenge
"Creating a sense of urgency that *all* students will achieve at high levels of learning, in *every* classroom, *every* day."

Best Reward
"When students and staff indicate they are *enjoying* learning."

University Professor Q & A

Cathie: You are in the business of training the next generation of school leaders—what's your leadership vision?

Gene: Today's and tomorrow's leaders need to be "leaders of learning." While you cannot lead if you cannot manage, leading a community of learners at the school and district level is the essential mission.

Cathie: How does accountability fit into your leadership preparation program?

Gene: Our program goals are to ensure that future superintendents and principals are leading a community of learners and that they are *accountable* for continuous improvements in staff and student learning. While the teacher is the greatest in-school factor associated with student learning, leadership at the building and district level is second in influence. Indeed, leadership *does* matter; it matters a great deal in building a culture of support for learning.

Cathie: You can't build that "culture of support" without teacher engagement. How do school leaders attain and sustain strong teacher involvement?

Gene: Highly effective leaders know schools that succeed practice distributive leadership. District and building leadership is not a one-person show; it is an orchestra of talent, all performing toward a common mission. The more the superintendent or principal meaningfully engages others, the greater the level of support and attainment of goals. Leaders of learning know the work is too challenging to go it alone. These leaders practice meaningful distributive leadership, in which everyone has the opportunity to lead learning.

Cathie: Giving teachers the opportunity to lead learning is a powerful concept. How does it unfold in schools?

Gene: Principals embed participatory leadership through building a common vision of student and staff learning. Teacher participation can take the form of coaching; internships; professional development trainer; and committee, team, and learning-community leadership.

Cathie: Many teachers grab on to any chance to get involved. But others are resistant, especially when it comes to implementing new initiatives. What should a principal do about uninvolved teachers?

Gene: Often teachers are unaware of the expectations to join and actively participate in new initiatives. Consequently, their first reaction may be resistance due to the lack of purposeful communication on the part of leaders.

Cathie: What does purposeful communication look like?

Gene: Working with teachers in the development of a common and agreed-upon vision for the initiative is a necessary first step toward common understanding and support. The job of leadership is to communicate the need for a common understanding for the new initiative before the team can complete the tasks involved in implementing the intended outcomes. Effective leaders provide clarity around the initiatives. Much of the misunderstanding around—and resistance to—change initiatives is a result of a lack of effective communication and clarity of expectations at the *beginning* of the change process.

Cathie: You seem to see staff reluctance as just a normal part of that change process.

Gene: Many leaders confuse resistance to change with the challenge of managing transitions. Leaders typically have no trouble with change, as it is inevitable, whereas managing transitions can be more difficult.

Cathie: What are transition management pathways?

Gene: Strong communication, active listening, authentic avenues for engagement, and ongoing support are skills practiced by effective leaders to support transitions for staff and to manage transitions well.

Cathie: When teachers ignore change transitions, what's the bottom line?

Gene: If teachers are sabotaging new initiatives, leaders must have the moral courage to confront the teachers, clearly articulate the expectations, jointly set benchmarks for improvements, provide support, and monitor progress. The key is concise listening, respectful relationships based on trust, joint goal-setting, and accountability.

Gene gives school leaders who are facing staff obstacles solid advice. Help your teachers see themselves as a "community of learners" by building a shared vision, communicating explicit expectations, outlining transition steps, and collecting evidence that will serve as success benchmarks. If you are wondering how to put this plan into action—read on.

Subduing Change Challengers

Gene urges leaders to confront unsupportive teachers and his admonition should be taken to heart: when teachers avoid change, principals must take action. But first play Sherlock Homes—before intervening, try to determine the *type* of resistance you are confronting. Detection strategies should include the following:

- Observations (in classrooms, at professional meetings, during parent conferences, in hallways). Do you hear teachers making negative comments? Are teachers tuning out during faculty meetings? Has the implementation of a new program gone too slowly in some teachers' classrooms?
- Collections of evidence (student achievement data, parent conference participation levels, teacher attendance—including tardiness). Do students make progress? Has the quality of parent communications faded? Is the teacher frequently late or absent?
- Candid conversations (during goal conferences, postobservation meetings, after classroom visits, at principal-initiated "intervention" meetings). What growth-provoking goals has the teacher set? How is progress being monitored? Why has student performance taken a nosedive? Is the teacher facing outside distractions that the principal should know about?

As you collect and assess the information you have gathered, begin formulating response actions that align with the type of resistance you seem to be encountering. A menu of intervention suggestions follows:

For the Confused

For every teacher who appears confused about school goals, there are usually a dozen more flying under the radar. Your best bet is to catch the perplexed by tackling misunderstandings openly and intentionally at faculty meetings. This should be done through activities that get teachers discussing, analyzing, and applying expectations at the classroom level. For example, let's say there is a goal to "strengthen the instructional core." Working in pairs or small groups, teachers could translate the goal into teacher-friendly language (e.g., we will improve the effectiveness of our teaching), make a web that depicts instructional core components (e.g., courses, instructional frameworks, interim assessments), and list examples of classroom practice (e.g., we will explicitly identify learning targets at the start of every lesson). When the teacher-friendly goals, component webs, and classroom practices are shared, further discussion may ensue. This is healthy—discussions may bring clarity to a goal or, at the very least, precipitate revisions that make the goal more accessible. The next step is developing a transition plan that shows teachers how to move incrementally toward goal outcomes. The plan ought to include strategies that will help teachers become instructionally proficient, such as additional professional development; lists of research-based, aligned instructional materials; a student performance assessment plan; and opportunities for teacher coaching and collaboration.

For the Distracted

Identifying the variables that impinge performance comes first with distracted teachers. Their distractions may be revealed if you ask the right questions, are an empathetic listener, offer support, and have a reputation for keeping confidences. Preoccupied teachers usually feel relieved when they unload their burdens, whether their challenges are short-term, like being kept up at night by a colicky newborn, or long-term, such as caring for a parent diagnosed with dementia. Your second job is to offer support that might include—depending upon the circumstance—recommending the teacher for family medical leave; putting the teacher in touch with a community agency, such as a senior services center; or arranging for financial, psychological, or marital counseling through a district-provided employee assistance program. Finally, you need to help the teacher create a realistic plan that ensures that school responsibilities are met while the teacher attends to out-of-school obligations. Start by collaboratively reviewing your school district's evaluation criteria, the teacher's past performance levels, and previous goal plans. Then decide together which responsibilities can remain at maintenance level and which require stretch goals. Limit the teacher to the "critical few"—two or three goals that will have the most impact on student performance.

For the Discouraged

When teachers repeatedly fail to improve student performance, they might give up. These discouraged teachers may also feel professionally disgraced, which only makes matters worse. Embarrassed teachers are not likely to disclose their insecurities to supervisors, ask curriculum directors or other specialists for help, or collaborate with more effective peers. Discouraged teachers need a cheerleader who moves them from despair to hope by applauding strengths, identifying barriers to success, and mapping a roadway to success. This may include mentoring from a high-performing teacher they trust, intentional coaching from their principal or subject area specialist, and strategic professional development. "Strategic" here means that in-service is aimed at remediating specific deficits, like misaligned lesson plans, ineffective questioning techniques, or poorly crafted interim assessments.

For the Anxious

Skilled school leaders help teachers face bad news, like major student performance setbacks, without causing undue anxiety. Leaders achieve this balancing act by acknowledging problems in an open but matter-of-fact manner, sharing the responsibility for disappointing outcomes, and demonstrating an unshakable belief in everyone's capacity to learn, grow, and achieve. Equally important is creating a *plan*—a guaranteed strategy for reducing anxiety. Good plans move teachers away from unproductive worrying to positive action. In the case of declining test scores, a solid plan ought to include identifying current strengths and successful practices, pinpointing variables that either support or negate strong student performance, and applying high-leverage strategies to weak areas. For example, let's say state assessment results show more students benchmarking in reading but fewer demonstrating proficiency in writing. Was the reading increase the result of increased instructional time, a greater focus on discrete skills, more practice with state assessment formats, or something else? If teachers identify "discrete skill focus" as the prime variable, perhaps this approach could be extended to writing through more intentional mini-lessons coupled with ample practice. Teachers and principals should decide together which actions to put into play. Whatever the decision, the focus should stay fixed on the problem—not perceived failures—while constructively supporting teachers' efforts to find viable solutions.

For the Coasters

Underperforming teachers need a wakeup call and the principal is responsible for providing it. Interventions begin with a heart-to-heart conversation about performance. But first, a cautionary note: you may need to give advance written notice to the teacher and/or invite the teacher to bring union representation—check the teachers' bargaining agreement or ask your personnel director before taking action. When you do meet with the teacher, present your concerns in a straightforward manner and back up your assertions with unquestionable data. If you believe student performance is on a downward slide, for example, present several years' worth of declining scores to prove your point. It also helps to compare these results to grade-level, district, and state averages. When you gather information for your conference, however, cast a wide net. Look at the teacher's absentee report (e.g., is the teacher absent far more than other employees?), school service (e.g., does the teacher volunteer for after-school events or serve on school and district committees?), growth activities (e.g., does the teacher read professionally or regularly sign up for workshops, webinars, and the like?), and levels of parent contact (e.g., what percentage of parents come to conferences compared to the levels of more effective teachers?). Although some teachers may initially deny any problems, most will accept a well-supported verdict and ask for direction.

The next step for the school leader is to create—in collaboration with the teacher—an improvement plan that specifies a few doable goals (e.g., oral reading fluency levels will meet or exceed current levels), implementation activities (e.g., daily fluency practice, weekly fluency timings), and monitoring check points (e.g., meeting with the teacher twice monthly to review students' fluency scores). If the teacher disclosed distractions at home or feelings of discouragement, take these admissions into account as you choose interventions. The teacher might, for example, benefit from a mentor or visits to the classrooms of high-powered colleagues.

For the I-Centered and Saboteurs

There are distinct signs that foretell a failing school. Low test scores, poor staff morale, and out-of-control students are among the signals that denote system failure. Soon to follow is a pervasive discomfort among schoolhouse inhabitants that Lew Smith tags "internal dissonance" (2008, p. 51). Although the term sounds ominous, Smith argues that internal dissonance can be a compelling force for change if it drives educators to actively pursue something better for their schools. School leaders can generate internal dissonance by presenting their faculty with credible evidence that their school is underperforming. A comparison of the school's test results with those of higher-performing schools with similar demographics is usually all that it takes. Cognitive dissonance is an emotion experienced by individuals that is similar to the "internal dissonance" identified by Smith. In the field of psychology, cognitive dissonance denotes the uneasy feelings that people experience when their belief is at odds with their behavior.

For example, Mrs. Jones may *believe* that she is a good driver's education instructor, but when 50 percent of her students fail their motor vehicle tests, her belief about her teaching competency will be at odds with the reality of her instructional ineffectiveness. Cognitive dissonance may develop after teachers are presented with test results that show *their* students consistently perform below grade-level, school, district, and state averages.

I am not suggesting that principals metaphorically beat up their teachers, but an uncomfortable dose of reality can go a long way toward provoking needed changes. School leaders can use the concepts of internal and cognitive dissonance to shift the attitudes of I-centered teachers and saboteurs—especially when coupled with probing questions that reveal underlying causes and information that aids in the development of strategic improvement plans

For Every Change Challenger

"Capacity building," Fullan informs us, "involves developing the collective ability—dispositions, skills, knowledge, motivation, and resources—to act together to bring about positive change" (2005, p. 4). This observation should remind school leaders to take a team approach to improving teacher performance. Teaming begins with the school district superintendent, who, in the words of Gene Sharratt, "must provide the clarity, the support, and the authority for principals to fulfill the expectation that principals *will* provide instructional leadership." When this instructional leadership requires confronting substandard teacher performance, for example, the superintendent can support principals by serving as a knowledgeable sounding board as interventions are considered, sharing information gleaned from experience and professional resources, and providing funds for mentors, coaches, and professional development.

In addition to the superintendent, school leaders should seek help from other members of the administrative team. District directors and coordinators, for example, have knowledge, skills, and resources that can support personnel development efforts. Human resources managers will help principals decipher teacher contract language governing supervision and evaluation procedures; directors of teaching and learning can find teacher coaches or appropriate in-service opportunities; and special services coordinators might release grant funds for trainings or classroom visitations.

Change challengers run the gamut—from overt to covert—but whatever the form, their negative impact must be addressed. School leaders should resolutely approach teacher roadblocks with patience and persistence. This requires recognizing the underlying causes of teacher disengagement, understanding motivations—or the lack thereof, and flying in with appropriate interventions.

Wrap-Up: Confront Change Challengers

Key Concepts

- Teachers who are "change challengers" may include well-meaning teachers who are confused, distracted, discouraged, or anxious.
- Some teachers undermine school improvement efforts by coasting, being I-centered, or intentionally sabotaging mandates.
- The earlier teacher resistance is addressed, the faster the turnaround.
- School renewal confusion is evident when teachers cannot identify their school's mission, explain priority goals, or develop supportive professional development plans.
- Distracted teachers may be identified by lackluster student performance, late submissions of required reports, limited participation in professional meetings, and poor-quality products.
- An overanxious workforce worries excessively, feels overwhelmed, and experiences fear about failing to meet expectations.
- Coasters do the bare minimum to get by in their classrooms, complain when professional meetings are scheduled, and ignore opportunities to serve on substantive committees.
- I-centered teachers put themselves first, disregard evidence that questions their practice, and avoid collaborative opportunities.
- School renewal saboteurs include the holdouts, the cynics, the naysayers, and the whiners.
- School leaders can detect change challengers through observation, evidence collection, and candid conversation.
- Interventions should be tailored to the type of change challenger you are addressing.

Best Strategies

- Help confused teachers understand goals through in-depth discussion and authentic opportunities to apply new concepts.
- Create transition plans that show teachers how to move incrementally toward goal outcomes.
- Offer support to distracted teachers and follow-up with goal plans that are both effective and doable.
- Provide ongoing mentoring, coaching, and in-service for discouraged teachers.
- Reduce staff anxiety by recognizing professional strengths and applying successful approaches to weak areas.

- Intervene when teachers are coasting by communicating concerns, providing evidence of substandard performance, and developing improvement plans.
- Use the concepts of cognitive and internal dissonance to move I-centered teachers and saboteurs into the reform mainstream.

Steps to Success

- Most schools have teachers who fall into one or more of the change challenger categories. Use observation, data collection, and conversations to identify the teachers, categories, and appropriate interventions.
- Dr. Gene Sharratt gave examples of distributive school leadership. List the ways leadership is shared in your school. How could these roles be expanded to include more teachers?

Conclusion

> Everything in education should reflect the faces of young people and the hope for their futures. Every dollar spent, lesson planned, contract signed, test given, and committee meeting attended, should make an impact on real lives—futures being written.
> —Kimberly Barnes

In *Remember the Children*, Joanne Rooney describes the urgent social, emotional, and academic needs that children bring to the schoolhouse and persuasively argues that "real life kids must dominate our conversations" (2010, p. 88). This assertion falls in line with the outlook of the student-centered practitioners who were interviewed for this book. Lois Frank, for example, emphasized in regard to teachers "that *all* students are their responsibility and in their care: not my kids—their kids." Kelli Doherty supported this notion when she talked about teachers being "kid effective," and Tim Bartlett chimed in by advising that raising student achievement is "about putting a name and face with a problem."

It was with students in mind that I wrote *The 6 Keys to Teacher Engagement*. Like Gene Sharratt, I believe that teachers—and school leaders—can be "leaders of learning" and, like Valerie Anderson, that they can "make a difference" in their classrooms, in their schools, and in the lives of their students. This laudatory goal requires an internal standard of professional excellence, a strong engagement in the work of the school, and the attitudes and skills that were addressed in Keys 1 through 6:

Key 1: Create a Culture of Engagement

Teacher	School Leader
Demonstrates a passion for teaching Commits to helping all students Strives to perfect performance Evidences high involvement	Believes in shared leadership Communicates a clear vision Performs in an ethical manner Demonstrates skilled instructional leadership

Key 2: Get Organizationally Engaged

Teacher	School Leader
Demonstrates organizational engagement Embraces the school's mission Grows professionally Learns from successes and failures	Builds supportive school cultures Conveys high expectations Bases mission and outcomes on evidence Becomes an effective change agent

Key 3: Engineer Engagement

Teacher	School Leader
Supports the growth of colleagues Contributes to professional discussions Observes meeting norms Reflects on professional practice Applies new information	Elicits high teacher engagement Plans meetings thoughtfully Uses varied presentation strategies Clarifies meeting purpose and outcomes Shares new information with teachers

Key 4: Zero In on Best Practice

Teacher	School Leader
Demonstrates best practices skillfully Verifies student knowledge/skill acquisition Uses instructional frameworks Implements core programs with fidelity Gets results—students learn	Identifies best-practice teaching Understands strong vs. weak research Uses evidence to choose programs Stays current with educational developments Demonstrates best practices

Key 5: Tap into Teacher Leadership

Teacher	School Leader
Demonstrates leadership potential Takes on leadership responsibilities Responds to leadership coaching Contributes to the growth of other teachers Supports the school mission and goals	Gains the trust and confidence of teachers Recruits teacher leaders Prepares teachers for leadership roles Assigns strategic tasks to lead teachers Recognizes teacher leader accomplishments

Key 6: Confront Change Challengers

Teacher	School Leader
Embraces reform measures Handles change transitions Understands the school's mission and goals Supports the school leadership's efforts	Creates a community of learners Identifies change challengers Determines change challengers' motives Confronts, then supports, uninvolved teachers

The foregoing lists of competencies for teachers and school leaders go hand in hand. They are interdependent, mutually supportive, and, in the words of Carol Fusek, "assist participants in a learning experience"—an *invaluable* learning experience through which teachers grow professionally, become powerfully engaged, and by virtue of their heightened competence and commitment unlock the doors to top teacher performance. Reason enough to share the promising concepts and skills captured in *The 6 Keys to Teacher Engagement*.

References

Barth, R. S. (2003). *Lessons learned: Shaping relationships and the culture of the workplace*. Thousand Oaks, CA: Sage.

Calkins, L. M., & Harwayne, S. (1991). *Living between the lines*. Portsmouth, NH: Heinemann.

Collins. (2001). *Good to great: Why some companies make the leap and others don't*. New York, NY: HarperCollins Publishers.

Copland, M. A., & Knapp, M. S. (2006). *Connecting leadership with learning: A framework for reflection, planning, and action*. Alexandria, VA: ASCD.

Council of Chief State School Officers (CCSSO). (2008). *Performance expectations and indicators for educational leaders*. Washington, DC: Author.

Danielson, C. (2006). *Teacher leadership that strengthens professional practice*. Alexandria, VA: ASCD.

Danielson, C. (2007). *Enhancing professional practice: A framework for teaching* (2nd ed.). Alexandria, VA: ASCD.

Dufour, Richard, Dufour, Rebecca, Eaker, R., & Many, T. W. (2006). *Learning by doing: A handbook for professional learning communities at work*. Bloomington, IN: Solution Tree Press.

Ellis, A. K. (2005). *Research on educational innovations*. Larchmont, NY: Eye On Education.

Elmore, R. (2008). Improving the instructional core. Retrieved from www.acsa.org/MainMenuCategories/ProfessionalLearning/CoachingMentoring/LeadershipCoaching/Coach-Resources/Elmore-Summary.aspx.

Farmer, L. (2011). Evaluation is a year round endeavor. *Principal News, 41*(1), 5.

Frank, L. (2011). Interview responses. Unpublished e-mail.

Fullan, M. (2005). *Leadership and sustainability: System thinkers in action*. Thousand Oaks, CA: Corwin Press.

Fullan, M. (2008). *The six secrets of change: What the best leaders do to help their organizations survive and thrive*. San Francisco: Jossey-Bass.

Glickman, C. D., Gordon, S. P., & Ross-Gordon, J. M. (2007). *SuperVision and instructional leadership: A developmental approach* (7th ed.). Boston: Pearson Education.

Goleman, D. (2006). *Social intelligence: The revolutionary new science of human relationships*. New York: Random House.

Goleman, D., Boyatzis, R., & McKee, A. (2002). *Primal leadership: Realizing the power of emotional intelligence*. Boston: Harvard Business School.

Guskey, T. R. (2010). Mastery learning. *Educational Leadership, 86*(2), 53–57.

Hartley, L. P. Quote: *The past is a foreign country; they do things differently there*. Retrieved from http://thinkexist.com/quotation/the_past_is_a_foreign_country-they_do_things/14056.html.

Kimball, S. M. (2011). Principals: Human capital managers at every school. *Phi Delta Kappan, 92*(7), 13–18.

Marshall, K. (2008). Interim assessments: A user's guide. *Phi Delta Kappan, 90*(1), 64–68.

Marzano, R. (2003). *What works in schools: Translating research into action.* Alexandria, VA: ASCD.

Marzano, R. (2007). The art and science of teaching: A comprehensive framework for effective instruction. Alexandria, VA: ASCD.

Marzano, R. (2009). Setting the record straight on "high yield" strategies. *Phi Delta Kappan, 91*(1), 30–37.

Marzano, R. (2010). *Formative assessment and standards-based grading.* Bloomington, IN: Solution Tree Press.

Mayes, F. (1996). *Under the Tuscan Sun.* New York, NY: Broadway Books.

McDonald, J. P., Mohr, N., Dichter, A., & McDonald, E. C. (2003). *The power of protocols: An educator's guide to better practice.* New York: Teachers College Press.

McEwan, E. K. (2002). *10 traits of highly effective teachers: How to hire, coach, and mentor successful teachers.* Thousand Oaks, CA: Corwin Press.

McEwan, E. K. (2005). *How to deal with teachers who are angry, troubled, exhausted, or just plain confused.* Thousand Oaks, CA: Corwin Press.

McEwan, E. K. (2009). *10 traits of highly effective schools: Raising the achievement bar for all students.* Thousand Oaks, CA: Corwin Press.

Merriam-Webster's Collegiate Dictionary (11th ed.). (2008). Springfield, MA: Merriam-Webster.

Northouse, P. G. (2004). *Leadership: Theory and practice.* Thousand Oaks, CA: Sage.

Ogawa, R. T. (2005). Leadership as a social construct: The expression of human agency within organizational constraint. In F. W. English (Ed.), *The Sage handbook of educational leadership: Advances in theory, research, and practice.* Thousand Oaks, CA: Sage.

Owens, R., & Valesky, T. C. (2007). *Organizational behavior in education: Adaptive leadership and school reform* (9th ed.). Boston: Pearson Education.

Peter, L. J. (1977). *Peter's quotations: Ideas for our time.* New York: William Morrow.

Ratey, J. J. (2008). Spark: The revolutionary new science of exercise and the brain. New York: Little, Brown.

Reeves, D. B. (2008). *Reframing teacher leadership to improve your school.* Alexandria, VA: ASCD.

Richardson, J. (2011). The ultimate practitioner. *Phi Delta Kappan, 93*(1), 27–32.

Roget's International Thesaurus (6th ed.). (2001). New York: Harper-Collins.

Rooney, J. (2010). Remember the children. *Educational Leadership, 67*(7), 88–89.

Sergiovanni, T. J. (1992). *Moral leadership: Getting to the heart of school improvement.* San Francisco: Jossey-Bass.

Shannon, G. S., & Bylsma, P. (2007). *The nine characteristics of high-performing schools: A researched-based resource for schools and districts to assist with improving student learning* (2nd ed.). Retrieved from www.k12.wa.us.edu/research/pubdocs/NineCharacteristics.pdf.

Smith, L. (2008). *Schools that change: Evidence-based improvement and effective change leadership.* Thousand Oaks, CA: Corwin Press.

Steel, J. L., & Boudett, K. P. (2008/2009). The collaborative advantage. *Educational Leadership, 66*(4), 54–59.

Tomlinson, C. A. (2005). *The differentiated classroom: Responding to the needs of all learners.* Upper Saddle River, NJ: Pearson-Merrill Prentice Hall.

West, C. E. (2009). Teaming up for student achievement. *Principal News, 38*(3), 28–29.

West, C. E. (2011a). Power-up your staff meetings. *Principal News, 40*(3), 10–11.

West, C. E. (2011b). *Problem-solving tools and tips for school leaders.* Larchmont, NY: Eye On Education.

West, C. E., & Derrington, M. L. (2009). *Leadership teaming: The superintendent-principal relationship.* Thousand Oaks, CA: Corwin Press.

West, C. E., & Frank, L. (2010). Climbing higher: Mountain Way Elementary. *Washington State Kappan, 4*(2), 18–21.